BEFORE MEMORIES FADE

BEFORE MEMORIES FADE

Memories of World War II; My Uncle and Men of the 10th Infantry Regiment of the 5th Infantry Division

By MELVIN H. DICK

NEW FORUMS
Stillwater, Oklahoma
U.S.A.

NEW FORUMS PRESS INC.

Published in the United States of America
by New Forums Press, Inc.
1018 S. Lewis St.
Stillwater, OK 74074
www.newforums.com

Copyright © 2011 by New Forums Press, Inc.

All rights reserved. No part of this publication may be reproduced or transmitted in any form or by any means, electronic or mechanical, including photocopy, or any information storage or retrieval system, without permission in writing from the publisher.

Library of Congress Cataloging-in-Publication Data Pending

This book may be ordered in bulk quantities at discount from New Forums Press, Inc., P.O. Box 876, Stillwater, OK 74076 [Federal I.D. No. 73 1123239]. Printed in the United States of America.

ISBN 10: 1-58107-208-2
ISBN 13: 978-1-581072-08-2

CONTENTS

FOREWORD .... *vii*
  1. CHRISTMAS 1944 1
  2. MAN FROM OKLAHOMA 3
  3. MEN OF THE 10th REGIMENT 15
  4. COMBAT ENGINEER 28
  5. D-DAY 35
  6. NORMANDY 44
  7. BATTLE FOR METZ 51
  8. BATTLE OF THE BULGE 63
  9. GERMANY AND HOME 83
10. FRIENDS 96
11. COUSINS AT WAR 106
12. AFTERWORD 134
ACKNOWLEDGEMENTS 137
SOURCES 140

FOREWORD

This book was written to remember my Uncle, Private First Class Melvin W. Dunn. He was a member of General George Patton's 3rd Army, 5th Infantry Division and the 10th Regiment in World War II. He was killed during the Ardennes Offensive, better known as the Battle of the Bulge on January 28, 1945. Through some luck and research I have been able to find a few men who fought with him in the 10th Regiment. They have told me of their memories of the war and of the men with whom they fought. The men are all in their eighties and nineties, with fading memories of a war sixty plus years ago. Some memories however have not gone away and are quite vivid. The war was an important part of their lives and something they can never completely forget. Many of those who were in the war have died, limiting access to history of the war. I have found personal accounts to be the best as they were there, close to the daily happenings. Most never knew the big picture, this was the job of the Generals.

This book is not meant to be a concise history of the war. There is not much about the destruction of cities or the gory details of the wounding and killing of people. I am sure the men remember such things, but at this time of their lives don't wish to talk about it. The men have told me of events of the day the 5th Division came to Normandy in early July, 1944, across France to the German border, through the Battle of the Bulge, across the Rhine River and on through Germany to the end of the war in May, 1945. My Grandmother kept all of the letters my Uncle wrote to her during his service time. Because of security he was limited to what he could write about, but they tell of some of the hardship he endured.

The Americans who worked in defense plants, producing war materials and those serving in uniform have been called," The Greatest Generation." I do agree they qualify for the title. Most of the men and women in uniform were born from 1915 to 1924 and experienced the depression and that experience of life hardened them and prepared them for conditions they faced in the war.

I don't think many today understand the war and how much of the world was affected. At least fifty million people lost their life because of the war. The destruction of property was tremendous and it was years before reconstruction was completed in the war torn countries. It was impossible for life to return to normal in Europe. The American soldiers returned home, but were changed and for many it took years before the war left their daily thoughts. We owe a huge debt to those who served in the war and they deserve to be given our appreciation with rockets firing and trumpets playing.

Melvin H. Dick
August 2009
Enid, Oklahoma

History with its flickering lamp,
Stumbles along the trail of the past,
Trying to reconstruct its scenes,
To revive its echoes, and kindle
With pale gleams the passion
of former days.

>   Winston Churchill
>   November 1940

When you go home
Tell them for us and say
For your tomorrows
We gave our today

>   Unknown

Day is done,
Gone the sun,
From the hills, from the lake, from the skies,
All is well,
Safely rest,
God is nigh.

>   Taps

This book dedicated to the memory of:
PFC. Melvin Wallace Dunn
And to my parents,
Raymond and Ruth

1

CHRISTMAS 1944

It was Christmas Eve; snow covered the ground, trees and buildings. It would have been an ideal Christmas setting, except for the scream of artillery coming in and the earth shaking explosion that followed, sending shrapnel buzzing through the air like a swarm of bees. The chatter of machine guns could be heard along with rifle fire that was rapid at times and then would slow to a shot here and there.

When the shelling stopped, the call for medic's to tend the wounded was heard across the battlefield. Smoke from fires covered the area and choked those engaged in the fight. There was the smell of burning wood, oil from the tanks and trucks, cordite and human flesh. Not like any Christmas Eve most of us remember. Those who fought in the Battle of the Bulge in December 1944 would like not to remember Christmas Eve and Christmas Day, but it is an experience they can never forget.

Pfc. Jack Davis, a Medic with the 10th Infantry Regiment's 1st Battalion remembers well the war that was happening in December 1944. Late in the day of Christmas Eve, the 1st Battalion ran into shelling from the enemy and had to fall back to already dug foxholes. Night comes quickly in Europe during the winter and Pfc. Davis could hear a man screaming from pain. He realized it was a German soldier and he was lying a few yards in front of his foxhole. After about one hour of listening to his cry of pain, he decided to crawl out and give him a shot of morphine. He did not want the enemy soldier to suffer. As a Medic, he carried morphine in collapsible tubes, called syrettes. The men close by provided cover for him and he crawled out and gave the man two or three shots. He did not try to treat the wound as it was apparent he was going to die. The man quieted down and was dead the next morning.

At a reunion of the 10th Infantry Regiment about fifty years later Pfc. Davis learned the entire story about the enemy soldier. A Sergeant in the 10th had captured him and while making him a prisoner had accidently shot the man. The bullet went through his stomach and cut a strap on Lt. Syd Lindsey's musette bag. Lt. Lindsey was behind him at the time and lucky to have been missed. Lt. Lindsey told Pfc. Davis at the reunion the prisoner and the man he crawled out to help in the dark of Christmas Eve was the same person.

Lt. Harold Storey, Commander of C Company of the 1st Battalion, and a group were looking for a place to sleep in a barn when his name was called. He and a few others had received Christmas packages. His was a box of cookies, which by this time were mostly crumbs. The crumbs were good and did not last long as he shared them with others. It was the only Christmas package he would receive for Christmas 1944.

My Uncle Pfc. Melvin Dunn was also a member of the 10th Regiments C Company. In a letter written to his mother on December 28, he writes, "Hope you all had a Merry Christmas. I spent Christmas Eve and Christmas Day in a foxhole. It was very cold; we have had snow on the ground for more than a week. Our Christmas dinner was on the 27th, was a little late, but we had turkey and all the trimmings. I hope to be home for next Christmas." He would not be home next Christmas or any Christmas. He spent his last Christmas in a war in the snow and cold of Northern Luxembourg.

2

MAN FROM OKLAHOMA

Melvin Wallace Dunn was an Oklahoma boy born June 30, 1923 at Mulhall, Logan County, Oklahoma. He was the sixth child of William Melvin and Mary Alice [Wilder] Dunn. My mother was a sister, about five years older. He grew up on a farm, learning to till the soil and care for animals. He attended a one room school, Pleasant View. One room schools with grades one through eight were common in rural Oklahoma and existed up to the end of World War II. Many at the time never went more than the first eight years.

Mulhall was a typical small town in rural Oklahoma during the 1930's and 40's and was the hub of activities for him and his family. The town supplied their need for food, clothing, entertainment, fuel to operate cars and some farm equipment, along with a Doctor to care for their health. Mulhall was a small town, like many in rural areas of the country. It sprang up after the land run in 1889. After a few short years the town had most of the businesses necessary to supply the needs of the farm families in the area. Mulhall was a close knit community. As children grew up and got married they did not move far from their family and friends. Children were taught, what today is referred to as old fashioned values. Life was simple, most did not have amenities such as indoor plumbing and electricity and homes were heated with wood or coal. Families were large and all had to work and contribute to the daily needs.

The family always called Melvin Wallace by his middle name and he has been Uncle Wallace to me. I never knew him well as I was six years old when I last saw him in the summer of 1943.

By Melvin Dick

In the early 1940's Mulhall was a thriving town with grocery stores, four places to get your automobile repaired, a bank, hotel, doctor's office, jail, ice house and drug store. Places of worship were also in Mulhall and some exist today. There was other business, some not lasting long. The town merchants pooled their money and provided a free movie on Saturday night, weather permitting as it was an outdoor screen.

In reading the letters Uncle Wallace wrote to his mother during the war, I was able to know he was in Mulhall on many occasions. He writes about seeing his friend Junior Hyde and movies that he saw again in England or that he talked with Bill Cothern, father of his boyhood friend Hubert. I am sure he went to Rundells Drug store and had ice cream, setting at the marble counter talking with other young people. Curtis Farmers Store was a popular gathering place for families, especially

Pfc. Melvin Wallace Dunn. Courtesy of the author.

on Saturday afternoons when some youngster drew a name for a free sack of groceries. I drew the name a few times and got to pick some candy from the candy case. Candy was kept in a glass cabinet in bread pans and I got to pick what I wanted. A small sack of candy was a real treasure at the time, but I had to share it with my sisters. I am sure I guarded that candy as if it were a treasure worth a million dollars. Uncle Wallace may have went up the street to watch as the men of the community pitched horseshoes in the vacant lot north of the Huffer Brothers Service Station on the west side of main street. My grandfather liked homemade ice cream and they stopped at the ice house to get ice to make the ice cream. I remember the times at my grandparents and how good the ice cream tasted.

Mulhall had a beautiful bank made of rose colored rock. It was on the corner on the west side of Main Street. The bank is a nice restaurant today and people come from far away to eat the good food that is served or see the walls full of photographs of early day Mulhall. Lucille Mulhall was a working cowgirl and many photos are of her roping a steer or participating in her father's Wild West show. On one wall is a large portrait of Lucille and Will Rogers. On a recent visit to Mulhall, I noticed a sign in front of the restaurant, POW/MIA's Not Forgotten. The sign does not refer to World War II, but to a war fought twenty five years later. To those that lost family in any war it is a reminder and brings tears. It means to convey the thought that none are forgotten and was put there by a caring person.

On the north end of town is a softball field. In the 1930's and 40's it was for baseball and many games were played on the part grass and dirt field. It was not like the fields of today and many players got a grounder in the face because of the rough ground, but it provided for fun and entertainment for the people of the Mulhall community. The field is named for one of its supporters in the 1940's, Walt Kincaid. Walt was a large man and operated a service station on the east side about one block from the field that now bears his name. He did not miss many games in his life.

Railroad tracks go through the town and have since the early 1900's. There was a station on the west side of the tracks and passenger and freight trains came through several times per day. In addition to passengers the trains carried mail. There were times when no passengers were on board and the train did not stop. The mail would be placed on an arm along one side of a car. A steel post with a hook would catch the mail sack. The system worked well. Uncle Wallace rode a train from this station when he left for service with the army. The same tracks brought him home on furlough and returned him back to duty. I would guess all the men from the Mulhall community rode trains to war. The station is no longer there and trains do not stop these days. Only the whistle can be heard at the crossing north of town and again at a crossing south of town. There is no evidence anyone remembers the young men who waited with their families in the station or on the brick platform outside for the train to take the sons of the community to war. The same tracks also returned them home after the war. The buildings with the brick platform were torn down many years ago. My Uncle Fred McNeill bought the bricks to build a new home, which was destroyed in a tornado in 1999. The tracks remain today and are the only reminder of what once was. Most of the men who rode the train from Mulhall to war are gone now and with them the memories of a time long passed.

Mulhall is not the same town today. The old buildings are gone and Uncle Wallace would not recognize the town. A tornado wrecked most of the building and homes in May 1999, but some new homes and business building have been replaced. Mulhall like most small towns of the 1940's is about gone, as the world changed, it could not keep pace.

Uncle Wallace had a girlfriend, Myrna Jean, who, according to his letters, wrote to him every day. She also sent Christmas presents and other packages of things such as stationary, tooth powder, soap and candy. I am not sure what happened to her after the war.

A cousin, Margie Anthis, remembers Uncle Wallace was fun to be with. He had a ready smile and cheerful attitude. He sometimes sang while doing work around the farm. She tells about the time he was hiding Easter eggs for the younger children and caught his foot on a wire, almost buried in the ground. The wire came up and caused a bad cut on the corner of his mouth. She can see this scar in the pictures taken while he was in the army.

Faye, a younger sister remembers him having a horse named Colonel. He often went riding with a neighbor, Hubert Cothern. Riding was common in those days and was a means of transportation for many. Most families, if they were lucky only had one car. Faye said, "He really loved that horse."

Wayne Murphy, a friend two years younger than Uncle Wallace was not accepted for service in World War II, but served in the Air Force during the Korean Conflict. Wayne's older sister married Cecil, Uncle Wallace's older brother. Wayne wrote many letters to Uncle Wallace during the war. I talked to Wayne about his days as a young man and how he knew Uncle Wallace. He said to me with a serious look on his face, "Melvin he was a good guy." Uncle Wallace mentions Wayne several times in his letters. The years have dulled Wayne's memory of the content of his letters. It brought a chuckle when I told him Uncle Wallace wrote saying, "Wayne keeps me up to date on everything back there from A to Z."

The war years brought rationing to all in America. Gasoline, tires, and food stuff was rationed. Things such as sugar, flour, salt and fresh meat were a few of the food stuffs rationed. As we often did not have sugar, I remember using white syrup on my oatmeal for breakfast. Farmers were fortunate in that they could raise many things on the farm and were not bothered about meat and vegetables that were on the list of things rationed. Families were issued a small book of stamps and one had to give a stamp at purchase or go without. The books were issued once a month and when your stamps were used up; you had to wait for the next issue.

Tires for the automobiles were very hard to get. None were kept in stores and orders were taken and time would pass before the tires came. The government maintained the warehouses of tires and closely controlled distribution. Farm communities like Mulhall probably fared better than the large cities.

A copy of Uncle Wallace's driver license has survived the years. It was issued in January 1942 and shows he was eighteen years old, six foot tall and weighed 157 pounds with brown hair and eyes. Not many people were six foot tall in those days and pictures of his platoon show him to have been one of the taller ones.

Both my Grandparents were of Irish Heritage, so Uncle Wallace was very Irish. I think it is ironic that he spent eight months in Northern Ireland training for combat.

Uncle Wallace's service time lasted for two years. In that time he wrote 88 letters to his mother. After he was assigned to the 10th Regiment of the 5th Infantry Division, all his letters were censored for security reasons. He was limited in things he could write about, not able to tell his mother what he was doing. Censoring was the job of the Junior Officers of his company. Lt. Harold Storey signed several and said, "Censoring letters of those he knew had been killed in combat was hard for me." Uncle Wallace could not tell his mother where in Northern Ireland he was and could not comment on the weather. His letters never mentioned being sick, or that he was wounded, even slightly during combat. He received lots of mail and packages from his mother, sisters and friends. Several times he ask his mother to send such things as candy, shaving soap, hair oil, tooth powder and other things he could not get at the Army PX. He was upset because the mail did not come in an orderly fashion and tried hard to find ways of improving it. Air-Mail was the best and would arrive in seven days, Oklahoma to Ireland. The letters often ask about the health and well being of the family and he sent pictures to his mother and others as often as possible. The letters do show how the war changes him as one would expect.

Uncle Wallace entered the Army on February 9, 1943 and went to Fort Sill, Oklahoma, and remained there for about two weeks. On February 22nd, he was on the way to Camp McCain Mississippi for basic training. Camp McCain at Grenada is located 100 miles south of Memphis, Tennessee. Thousands of men were trained for World War II at Camp McCain. The camp was established in 1942, was built quickly and was typical of many. The buildings were two stories and had only one board thick siding. Nothing was included for comfort, only the bare minimum; one could stay dry, but not warm and did not have a cooling system. The camp is a National Guard Training center today and living conditions have been greatly improved.

Uncle Wallace began serious training at this time by learning to wear uniforms and to march at the command of the Drill Sergeant. He had training in weapons and marched many miles each day. He was busy almost day and night. One letter complained of the food and he wanted to leave Camp McCain and go some other place soon. He had to get along on little food that was not good and did not get much sleep. He was doing things he did not like and could not understand the reason for any of it.

He learned that meal time in the Army was not breakfast, lunch and dinner, but was chow time. All soldiers have always been concerned about what was served at chow. SOS was slang for a breakfast meal. It was chip beef and white gravy served on toast, does not sound bad, but the Army could mess it up. Liquid fat was at least ten inches deep on the serving pot and that usually took away ones appetite.

In June 1943 Uncle Wallace wrote about the possibility of getting a furlough starting sometime in July. Junior Hyde, his friend from Mulhall was also at Camp McCain and must have been a few weeks ahead in training had gone on furlough and returned and told him it did not take long to get home by train. His next letter was written on October 10th and I believe he had been home for thirty days, then returned to Camp McCain and was sent to Fort Meade, Maryland. The next letter was on October 15th and said he could not say where he was, but not to worry if they did not hear from him any time soon. No records are available on troop shipment to Europe for October 15, to the 20th in 1943. Uncle Wallace probably left the USA from either Fort Hamilton or Camp Shanks in New York. Camp Shanks was the shipping point for about two million troops during the war. It was authorized to be constructed in 1942 and was completed by May 1943 and was known as, Last Stop USA. All soldiers had to have all their equipment before boarding and were responsible for keeping it until they were assigned to a camp in Europe. The ships were crowded with troops and all the equipment made living conditions worse.

Ships transporting troops from New York usually took about fourteen days. Most had escort ships protecting them, but the ships had to maintain an irregular course to keep enemy Submarines from finding them. A letter dated November 4th, tells about the trip over and the fact he never was seasick. Seasickness was a great problem for most. Uncle Wallace wrote his mother that he did not get seasick, something to be proud of at the time. Those who did get seasick could not keep food down, could not sleep and were miserable until they were on land in Europe. Uncle Wallace did not say where in England he was stationed, but was probably at Tidworth Barracks, near Amesbury. Tidworth Barracks was a stopping place for those going to Europe until they were assigned to a Division or the Division moved to a permanent place for training. He thought the food was good and enjoyed a free movie each night.

Uncle Wallace was assigned to the 5th Infantry Division and sent to Northern Ireland. The Infantry Divisions in World War II contained three Regiments and He was sent to the 10th Regiment. The 10th was billeted in or near Newcastle, not far from the east coast and about fifty miles from Belfast. He was a member of the 1st Battalions C Company, 1st Platoon. He met his first Platoon Leader, Lt. Jack Garner. He also came to know Sgt. Gus Reinhart. Sgt. Reinhart was a good soldier and a special person.

The country in Northern Ireland is rugged with hills and valleys. It provided an excellent site for combat training. Lt. Ralph Cupelli, a Platoon Leader in C Company, told me about a typical day in training. He said, "We were up early, had breakfast and then marched five miles and ran the last 500 yards." Lt. Cupelli remembers the hills and thought they always went up and never down. They once did a thirty six mile march and everyone was in good physical shape. Lt. Cupelli said, "I later learned that being in good shape and handling combat was two distinctly different things."

Lt. Cupelli remembers going to dances at the Hotel Slevie Donard on Saturday nights in Newcastle. They had a nice time. The Hotel still exist today. Women would ride the train from the towns in the area and dance with the soldiers. Nylon stockings were not available and most of the women painted a substance on their legs to simulate stockings and it would run when it became wet. I have visited Ireland and learned that Slevie means ridge top mountains. The mountains in Ireland are not like our Rocky Mountains, but to run and walk over them carrying a pack and rifle would require a lot of physical strength.

The army social life was different for officers and enlisted men. They never did anything together or at the same place and time. The officers were paid a lot more and could afford some luxury. The enlisted men did have the opportunity to attend dances. PFC Jack Davis remembers some of the times they were on pass and what happened. Those who drank a lot always seemed to get a fight started and several would be sent to the medics to get patched up before the weekend was over.

Almost nothing is evident today to remind us the 5th Infantry Division was in Northern Ireland. The training sites have disappeared and few people would remember the great number of soldiers that once were part of the daily life around Newcastle. If the walls of the Slevie Donard Hotel could talk they might tell us of the romances, the one night stands of young people living in an uncertain world. The Slevie Donard Mountains may remember the sound of young soldiers bitching about all the marching, the weight of packs and the long hours of training. Some who were there might tell stories if they want

Pfc. Dunn with unknown buddy in Ireland. Courtesy of the author.

to remember after almost seventy years. Time has erased the evidence and fading memories will leave us only guessing about the real truth.

Uncle Wallace wrote many letters while in Northern Ire-

Above: Gen. George Patton speaking to the men of the 10th Regiment in Ireland. Courtesy of the Society of the Fifth Division.

Right: Pfc. Melvin Dunn on pass in Ireland. Courtesy of the author.

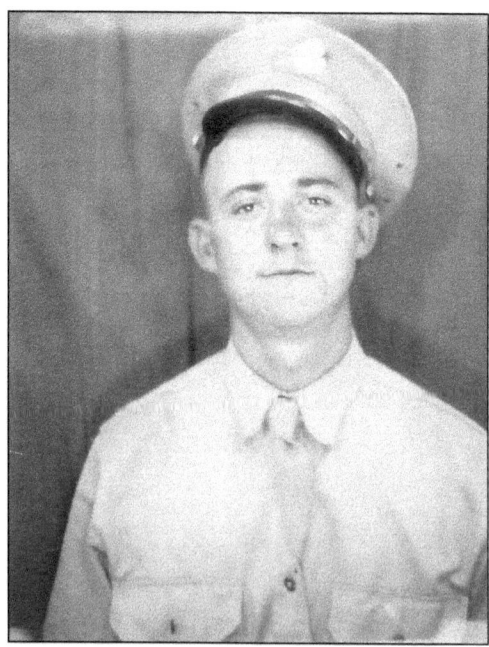

land. He asked his mother how many cows they were milking and did she plan to have lots of chickens next spring. He wanted his mother to get Christmas presents for the younger children and his girlfriend. He wanted her to wish everyone Merry

Col. Robert Bell, Commander of the 10th Regiment. Courtesy of the Combat Narrative of the 10th Regt. in WW2.

Lt. Col. William Breckinridge, Exc. Officer of the 10th Regt. Courtesy of the Combat Narrative of the 10th Regt. in WW2.

Christmas and he hoped to be home for next Christmas. One letter told her, "This is something you really want to know, but four star General Eisenhower came to visit us."

He got passes to Belfast at least two times and told his mother he did not like it there. No place was as good to him as the old USA. The places he visited in Europe were not home and he wanted to be with his family. In a letter written on Sunday, he makes an apology for not going to church that morning because he slept in, but assures her he will go that evening.

The training in Ireland was intense, the men learned to work as a Platoon, a Company and a Battalion. They were taught to defend and attack. Friendships were formed and many lasted for a lifetime.

3

MEN OF THE 10TH REGIMENT

The men of World War II are leaving us at the rate of more than 1000 per day. It is becoming difficult to find them. Some will not talk about their experiences and shy away from writers or reporters asking questions. The men of the 10th Regiment of the 5th Infantry Division were a bit reluctant to talk with me in the beginning, but as they came to know me started telling more stories about their time in the war. I sent out a form letter to several whom I knew served in C Company and received telephone calls almost immediately. I will never be able to repay them for the gracious way they have treated me over the last few years.

Time has taken away some of their memories and I think they suppress some things that are too difficult to talk about. I respect the right of those who did not answer the letter to remain silent. Some have wounds that have never completely healed and their activity has been restricted for all the years since the war. The sights, sounds and smells of the battlefield will not go away and memories return without their permission.

To those of us who raised our right hand and repeated the oath, I believe a brotherhood was formed. It makes no difference when one served. The language of the military has been mostly the same for many years and we all understand one another.

Reunions have kept former soldiers in touch. Relationships formed during their service time have lasted. They remained friends, buddies, helping each other through difficult times. They came to know each others families and gave unfailing support.

Lt. Ralph Cupelli from Pennsylvania is a graduate of Penn State University, where he went through the Reserve Officers Training Corps, receiving a commission as 2nd Lieutenant. Lt. Cupelli joined the 10th Regiment in Iceland in July 1942. The 10th Regiment was ordered to Europe in August 1943. Lt. Cupelli was leader of the 3rd platoon of C Company until he was wounded at Metz in September 1944. He returned to the Regiment in December after recovering from his wound. He did not serve with C Company, but was in Regiment Headquarters working in Intelligence and Reconnaissance. I believe his heart was always with C Company and after the war attended many of the company reunions. He will never forget the date the Division arrived in Normandy as it was one day after his twenty fourth birthday.

After the war Lt. Cupelli returned home, was married and worked for U. S. Steel in accounting until he retired. He and his wife Aimee have five children and three grandchildren. Like many of the men of World War II, Lt. Cupelli joined the reserves and retired as a Lieutenant Colonel. In 1961 several Reserve Units were called to active duty and Lt. Cupelli's unit and the unit I belong to were both stationed at Fort Sill, Oklahoma. We did not know each other at the time and would meet after more than forty years.

Lt. Cupelli has returned to France and to Arnaville where he was wounded. The French Government awarded him the French Fourragere. He now has two as the 5th Division received the award for service in the war.

Lt. Byron E. Liebner was from Wisconsin and was active in the sports programs in high school, playing basketball and football. He attended the University of Wisconsin at Madison after high school and played basketball. During his freshman year they won the National Championship. After entering the Army on June 19, 1943, he played basketball and football for the Army and had the opportunity to know many of the great athletes of the early 1940's. Bob Waterfield played football professionally for the Rams and when in the Army he was the quarterback and Lt. Liebner the running back. The Army had all the good players and none were left to give them much competition. Lt. Liebner became bored with sports and wanted to do something to aid the war effort. He attended the Officer Candidate School and was commissioned a 2nd Lieutenant of Infantry. He left for Europe on March 17, 1944 and was assigned to C Company of the 10th Regiment.

Lt. Liebner was leader of the 2nd platoon of C Company when the Regiment entered combat in Normandy. He was wounded while leading a patrol in late July, but recovered after spending time in a hospital. In early December Lt. Liebner returned to C Company and was assigned as leader of the weapons platoon until being wounded again on January 22, 1945 during the Battle of the Bulge.

The war in Europe ended as he was returning to C Com-

Lt. Byron Liebner of C Company. Courtesy of Byron Liebner.

pany and he was ordered to Nice, France to command a Prisoner of War Camp. The POW's worked in a hospital cleaning floors, carrying bed pans and food trays. They often stole from the patients and had to be searched after each work period. For punishment they were sent to remove mines from the beach area. They complained and Lt. Liebner told them, "You put them there and now you must remove them."

Lt. Liebner began having trouble with his wounds and was evacuated to the states for further treatment. He spent many months in the Army Hospital in Clinton, Iowa before being separated from the Army in June, 1947. While in the hospital Lt. Liebner met Lt. Lucille Renken, an Army Nurse from Nebraska. Lucille was a farm girl and did Basic Training at Camp Carson, Colorado and was commissioned a 2nd Lieutenant in the Army Nurse Corps. She spent one year in the Army and all of it at the hospital in Clinton, Iowa. I ask her about her time in the Army and she told me she did not have a spectacular story to tell. Most do not have a spectacular story, but it was because they all did their jobs well that we were able to win the war. What she did to take care of the wounded is spectacular enough and deserves our special thanks.

Lt. Byron Liebner and Lt. Lucille Renken were married in January 1946. Lucille continued nursing while raising six children. She worked the evening shift while her husband was home caring for the children, retiring in 1986.

After the war Lt. Liebner returned to Wisconsin and a few years later bought the family business from his father. He and a good friend ran the business for almost forty years until he retired in 1984 and sold the business to his youngest son in 2000.

During the training time in Northern Ireland, Lt. Liebner noticed two men in his platoon who were older than the rest and recommended they be assigned less dangerous duties. One man was thirty nine and the other forty one. Col. Bell the Regiment Commander approved the recommendation.

Lt. Byron E. Liebner died May 1, 2007 after a battle with cancer. I knew he had not felt well for many months, but always was pleasant to talk with, relating stories of the war. Pfc. Jack Davis said, "We have lost a good man." I agree, another frontline warrior is gone. Their number is being reduced every day. Mrs. Liebner told me he talked about coming to see me and we could go to Oklahoma City, visit a friend and then go to dinner at the Cattlemen's Café. He thought they had the best steaks of any he had eaten. He had a great zest for life and told me one day when I called that he was going to a baseball game and watch his Grandson play. He said, "He will be disappointed if I don't come." I think Byron would have been disappointed also.

Harold Storey is from Georgia and a graduate of the University of Georgia. He began his time there on his seventeenth birthday. He went through the R.O.T.C. Program and was commissioned a 2nd Lieutenant in Infantry. He did not realize the job of a junior officer in the Infantry was very dangerous. He came to C Company in late July 1944 as a replacement officer and was assigned as leader of the 2nd platoon replacing the wounded Lt. Liebner. He thinks he was the only officer in a group of 250 men arriving at Utah Beach. While transferring

Capt. Harold Storey of C Company. Courtesy of Harold Storey.

C Company Platoon Leaders. Photo taken in Ireland in June 1944. L-R Lts. Ralph Cupelli, Carl Hansen, Byron Liebner and Gene Dille. Courtesy of Byron Liebner.

C Company Headquarters Personnel in Ireland June 1944. Front row L-R, 1st Stallbaum, 3rd Lentz, 4th Lt. Dille, 5th Capt. William Davis and 7th Kelly. Courtesy of Byron Liebner.

1st Platoon of C Company in Ireland June 1944. Front row L-R, 6th Lt. Jack Garner, 7th SSgt. Gus Reinhart. 2nd row 9th Pfc. Melvin Dunn. Courtesy of Byron Liebner.

2nd Platoon of C Company in Ireland June 1944. Front row, L-R, 6th Lt. Byron Liebner. Courtesy of Byron Liebner.

3rd Platoon of C Company in Ireland June 1944. Front row, L-R, 8th Lt. Ralph Cupelli. Courtesy of Byron Liebner.

Weapons Platoon of C Company in Ireland June 1944. Front row, L-R, 6th Lt. Carl Hansen. Courtesy of Byron Liebner.

from a large ship to boats that would take them ashore, equipment was lost and two men were hurt when their legs were caught between the small boat and the side of the big ship. They were let off in waist deep water and had to wade to shore.

Lt. Storey was leader of the 2nd platoon until after the river crossing at Arnaville. C Company was reduced to forty two men and one officer and Lt. Storey was then named Commanding Officer of C Company. Lt. Storey was CO of the company until seriously wounded on January 22, 1945 during the Battle of the Bulge. The wound ended the war for him as he spent the next several months in a hospital in England.

Lt. Storey has written of his memories of the war and sent copies of the stories to me. I ask him to write more about the battle for Metz and he finally agreed to do it. He once told me that to write about what he did in the war seemed self serving. Lt. Storey returned to Europe and to the river at Arnaville to see again where he fought. A lot of veterans have returned to the battle areas in their later years.

Frank V. Langfitt Jr. is a graduate of the University of West

Lt. Col. Frank V. Langfitt Jr. Commander of the 1st Battalion of the 10th Regt. Courtesy of Frank Langfitt.

Virginia after starting at the Virginia Military Institute, but transferred after two years. He like others received a commission after completing R.O.T.C. His first post was Fort Hays in Columbus, Ohio with the 10th Regiment's 1st Battalion, C Company and the 1st Platoon, the same as my Uncle served with. In 1941, he was part of the Tennessee Maneuvers, a massive training exercise. He said, "I was a very green 2nd Lieutenant at the time." He was to spend almost six years in the Army and all of the time with the 10th Regiment. Shortly before going to Normandy he was promoted to Lt. Colonel and Commander of the 1st Battalion. In early April, 1945 during a shuffle of Officers, Lt Col. Langfitt was promoted to executive Officer of the 10th Regiment. He returned to the states with the Division and was in a reserve unit for a short time, but felt five children and the demands of training requirements was more than he could keep up with. In one correspondence he wrote, "I have not been camping since the war." During the war had enough time in a sleeping bag, on the ground or hard floor and in a tent and wanted no more of the same.

Lt. Col Langfitt's generous gift of a copy of the History of the 10th Infantry Regiment in World War II, a book printed in 1946 and hard to find, made it possible for me to track the action of the Regiment during the war and know all the places my Uncle fought.

Pfc. John, "Jack" Davis grew up in Warren County New Jersey, but has spent most of his life in Easton, Pennsylvania. After the war he used the GI Bill to get a degree in Pharmacy. He thinks the GI Bill was one of the best things President Roosevelt thought of as it equalized the rich and poor when getting an education.

Pfc. Jack Davis was in D Company of the 10th Regiment, but often was assigned to C Company, where he had many friends during and after the war. C Company made him an honorary member after the war and I believe he is proud of this fact.

Pfc. Davis was a Medic and worked where needed, often assigned to other Company's during combat. He also carried ammunition for a machine gun section. A Medics job was dangerous and he wanted out of the Medical Corps. The Red Cross painted on the helmet was often used as a target by the enemy and he saw many of his fellow Medic's shot while treating wounded during a battle.

I asked Pfc. Davis about medals he received for action during the war and he was reluctant to talk about them. To him all the hero's are in the cemeteries. He fought in all five campaigns, was twice wounded, but refused to be evacuated. He called them only flesh wounds. He was recognized for action awarding him the Silver Star and Bronze Star, but does not want to talk about such things. He finally said. "I will tell you because I believe you understand." Very few in the Infantry were able to be in all five campaigns. He suffers to this day from the wounds and frozen feet and hands due to the very cold conditions during the Battle of the Bulge.

Pfc. Davis was very helpful as he knows the history of the war well. The other men all told me to contact him, "because he knows more than we do about what happened."

After the war Pfc. Davis returned home and married Mary Jane Luckenbach, a hospital nurse he had met before the war. They had four daughters and several grandchildren. Mary Jane died in 1983 after a long battle with cancer. He owned a Pharmacy in Easton from 1957 to 2002 and now belongs to the Lehigh Valley Chapter, Veterans of the Battle of the Bulge. He is proud to have served in the 5th Division's 10th Regiment and is a member of the Society of the 5th Division. Gen. Patton thought the best news at Christmas in 1944 was what the 10th Regiment did soon after arriving in Luxembourg, they went on the attack. The slogan of the 10th was, when it gets to tough for everyone else, it's just right for us. Pfc. Davis has lived by the slogan every day since the war.

Some writers of military history have interviewed Pfc. Davis and used his knowledge of history. Charles B. MacDonald, a historian for the Army and a veteran of the war consulted him. He is quoted in David P. Colley's book, SAFELY REST, about the return of the war dead.

One day while talking with Pfc. Davis I told him, "I was never given the final test." He said, "What do you mean?" "I was never in combat and don't know if I could do it." He replied, "You served didn't you." "Yes sir." This soft speaking voice became stern, "Don't think that and don't say that." My feelings ran away at that point and I felt good.

Staff Sergeant August Reinhart was from Ohio and a member of the C Company's 1st platoon with Uncle Wallace. I never spoke to him as he died in 1993 before I began research of C Company. He is included because of those who spoke about him. Pfc. Davis thinks he was the best soldier he saw in the war. Lt. Liebner probably knew him best and thought he was a very good soldier, a good communicator; always keeping everyone informed. He had tremendous admiration for Sgt. Reinhart and told me he was not wounded during the war despite the fact he continually exposed himself to the enemy. Lt. Liebner said, "I was always yelling at him to take cover." Lt. Liebner thought God was protecting him, except for one day after the war and Sgt. Reinhart was helping his father harvest nuts, fell from a tree breaking his back and was a paraplegic for the rest of his life.

Sgt Reinhart was captured at Putscheid and it is not clear what happened after that day. Most believe he spent time in a POW Camp near Hammelburg, Germany, but escaped and finished the war with the 103rd Infantry Division. Sgt. Reinhart would have been awarded a Battlefield Commission, if he had not been captured at Putscheid. Several times during the war when an officer was not available as Platoon Leader of the 1st Platoon, Sgt. Reinhart had taken charge and done the job. Sergeants' doing the job of Platoon Leader was common during the war in almost all Infantry Regiments.

Sgt. Reinhart was a great ambassador for the 10th Regiment and according to Lt. Ralph Cupelli was most responsible for the Regimental and Company reunions after the war. He drove around the country visiting his old army buddies or the families of those killed in the war. Brad Clover, son of Sgt. Bud Clover remembers him coming to visit his mother. He was always in a wheelchair, was very nice to them, but would not say much about the war. Mrs. Clover noticed Sgt. Reinhart's name was on something sent home with his father's affects and she wrote to the Army asking for an address. She wanted to know everything about her husband and wrote to Sgt. Reinhart asking questions.

Sgt. Reinhart worked for the John Deere Company after the war and was injured when a bottle of acid spilled on a table and ran down on his foot, causing a terrible wound. Sgt. Reinhart had a brother in the war and he too was not wounded, but after the war while working on a motorcycle, it fell killing him.

Sgt. Reinhart was a frequent guest in the Liebner home and they kept all the letters he wrote. When Sgt. Reinhart died in 1993, Lt. Liebner and his eldest son went to his funeral, attended by twelve men from C Company.

The men of the 10th Regiment and C Company all have told me they could have given me names of more men, if I had started five years earlier. The men and their memories are fading and the real stories of the war will remain with them and the history these men could have spoken about is lost.

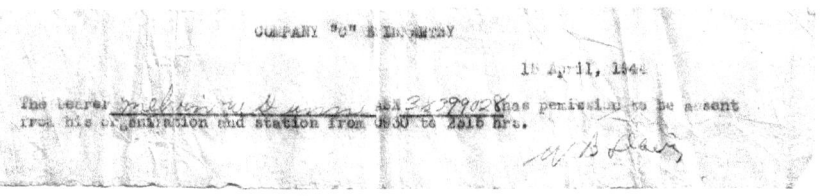

The pass issued to my uncle.

4

COMBAT ENGINEER

The combat engineers were an important group to all frontline units in World War ll. Among the many duties was clearing of the beach obstacles during amphibious operations, building roads to get wheeled vehicles off the beach and all across Europe, clearing mine fields, building or repairing bridges for the Infantry and other units during the fighting. They manned the boats during river crossings, making several trips which exposed them to enemy gun fire. In many instances they performed duties as Infantrymen to keep open the bridge they had just constructed. Writers of Military History have not written much about the Engineers. Division and Regimental histories mention the Engineers, but details are few. Most of the men assigned to the combat engineers had previously been employed in some kind of engineering job before the war. They scored high on the test each person was given on entering the service. During the Battle of the Bulge the Engineers performed well, blowing up bridges, disrupting the plans of the Germans and caused one German Tank Commander to exclaim, "Those Dammed Engineers!"

Tom Tucker was an Engineer and proud of it. He and his comrades were there to interrupt any and all plans of the German Army. Tom was born in Oklahoma in 1923, but moved to California as an infant and has resided there since. After high school Tom was employed by Convair Aeronautics as a tool designer on the Boeing B-24 Bomber. After being inducted into the Army he was assigned to the Engineers and took training at Camp Abbot, Oregon before being deployed to Europe. While home on leave Tom was married in January 1944 and shipped out two weeks later.

Tom, like more than two million others left Camp Shanks, New York bound for England aboard one of the many troop transport ships. After arriving in England, he was sent to a special school. He was there as a replacement and would later be assigned to the 5th Infantry Division's, 7th Combat Engineer Battalion, B Company. The 5th Division did not go to Normandy for the D-Day invasion. Tom said, "There was a rumor they did not need another Division in Normandy because the casualties were less than expected." Reality was the beach area could not hold any more men and equipment until the Allies pushed farther inland.

More men and equipment was needed, much more before the war was over and the 5th Division landed at Utah beach on July 9, 1944 and was assigned to the 3rd Army. It became apparent soon after landing that Tom was in the war and the many days of training was put to use. Tom remembers the bombing of St. Lo and the breakout, which took the 5th Division out of the beach head and started them across France. The 5th did some hard fighting at Hill 183, taking a high number of casualties. After the war Tom returned to Normandy and Hill 183. He said, "The hill did not look formidable, it was only another hill." There were no enemy guns firing the second time, no one trying to contain Tom and the others in Normandy. The Engineers were busy clearing mine fields and opening roads for traffic to move forward. The roads often were littered with German artillery, trucks, dead horses and soldiers as a result of the strafing and bombing by Allied aircraft and the shelling of Artillery units.

Angers was taken by the 5th Division and Tom remembers they were given shots, probably tetanus. In my interview notes I stated Angers was easily taken by the 5th. Tom responded by saying, "Combat was never easy." I meant to convey that casualties were light in the fighting at Angers. Tom was right to correct me.

The 5th division moved fast going across France driving the German army back to their border. One veteran thought they were used as Shock Troops, moving very fast, not having time for much sleep or hot meals. The next mission was the crossing of the Moselle River; near the French city of Metz. The Division had moved fast, outrunning the ability for supplies to keep up with the pace. The 5th had to stop and wait for supplies. Gasoline was the major problem as it took about 400,000 gallons per day to sustain operations of the 3rd Army.

The crossing of the Moselle was difficult and the Division suffered very high casualties. The 11th Regiment was selected to cross at Dornot and did make a crossing, but could not maintain positions due to high casualties and the fact no tanks could make it across to assist. The 11th was withdrawn and two days later the 10th Regiment made a crossing at Arnaville. The 11th helped by continued firing across the river, keeping the enemy busy. Casualties were as much as eighty percent for one Battalion of the 11th and the 10th Regiments C Company which started the crossing with two hundred and six officers and enlisted men were reduced to forty two men and one officer in the next two days. The area around Metz had several Forts made of reinforced concrete with tunnels going out to gun positions. Tom and other members of the 7th Combat Engineer

Cpl. Tom Tucker, 7th Combat Engineers in Luxembourg December 1944. Courtesy of Tom Tucker.

Battalion were in the tunnels for several days helping the Infantrymen. They used torches to cut through steel doors and removed mines and other explosives. In the confined space, fumes from the torches caused men to become sick. The 5th Division finally abandoned this tactic after several days.

Tom and other members of B Company were ordered to construct a foot bridge to cross the Seille River. They were to build the bridge on land, then place it across the river. It had been raining almost every day and the river was rising, making the river wider. The mission was accomplished. Metz was captured on November 21, 1944, about Thanksgiving Day.

The 5th Division moved on to the Saar Basin along the German border, doing some fighting, taking prisoners and training to attack the Siegfried Line or as it was commonly known, the West Wall. The Battle of the Bulge, which began on December 16, 1944, stopped the attack as the 5th was ordered to Luxembourg to assist the 4th Infantry Division. Tom's squad was in the small village of Heffingen. It had been snowing for a few days and was very cold. The squad was by a two story house and in a barn that had one wall shot away. The barn did not offer much protection from the snow and cold and the men wanted to be in the house with a fire. Luxembourg was a friendly country and the men could not take over the house. One man in the squad could speak German and the others urged him to talk with the owners, the Faber family and ask them for space to get in out of the weather. The house was occupied by a man and his wife with their three daughters. The family finally agreed to let them come in, but they could only be on the bottom floor. The family would live upstairs which had the only bathroom. Tom said, "We did not worry about a bathroom. We wanted out of the cold."

The house had one stove and it was downstairs. Tom said, "A railroad station was a little way down the road and it had some coal." The men brought back enough coal to heat the house for several days. The stove was about twelve inches square and eighteen inches high and was stacked three high. Tom said," We soon had a roaring fire, but it was too hot as we scorched the floor." The men got to know the Faber's well during their stay. Since the war Tom and his wife have returned many times to Luxembourg and always visited the Faber family. The Faber's have teased Tom about scorching the floor, never letting him forget that the house could have burned down. Today only two of the daughters are alive and they still own the house with the scorched floor. One of the daughters husband is a hair dresser for the Grand Duchy of Luxembourg and has been made a Knight of Luxembourg.

Tom also has a good friend living in Echternach, Fred Karen. Fred has studied the war in Luxembourg and can relate about the positions of the 5th Division. Fred now suffers from Parkinson's and is not able to walk well. In the past he could take one to the foxholes of the men and tell about the action that took place in the area.

The 5th division had pushed the German army back across the Sauer River and on January 18, 1945 they were ordered to cross the river. The Engineer's manned the boats and made several crossings in which they received Artillery fire making the crossing difficult. As they were preparing to cross, a tree burst killed Tom's good friend, Leroy Thomas, and three or four more. All river crossings were difficult, but this one was rated as about the worst.

The 5th continued to move north and push the German army out of Luxembourg. The snow was deep and the temperatures were down to single digits. This was not ideal conditions for fighting a war. Tom remembers being part of a group of four men that plowed open the road from Diekirch to Putscheid on the night of January 27, preparing for the attack on Putscheid the next day. The snow was knee deep and it was dark. One man would go in front of the dozer to locate the road, when he became tired another took his place. Tom has never understood how they managed to stay on the road. The road made a left turn as they neared Putscheid. A shot was fired at them by the feared 88 and Tom felt the shell went between his legs. They came to a farm house and went in to warm up, before returning to Diekirch. Officers of the 10th Regiment were in the house going over maps and preparing for the attack. Major Haughey, second in command of the 10th was one of the officers.

The 5th division moved to Berdorf and prepared to cross

the Sauer River again. The Engineer's were ordered to build a foot bridge, but never finished it. The crossing was made on the night of February 7th after all the divisions fire power had been brought forward. The crossing was at Wallerbach and only two boats got across, Tom's and one other. As Tom's boat was making the return trip, he was wounded by artillery fire and sent to a hospital in Luxembourg City. Tom heard a rumor that when wounded and your stay in the hospital was long, you would be sent back to another unit. Tom did not want to be with another unit and after two days talked to the Doctor and was allowed to return to his unit.

The 7th Combat Engineers of the 5th division helped with many river crossings and after Tom returned, the 5th was at Bollendorf and ready to cross the Prum River. During the crossing they were shelled for about thirty minutes and then the shelling stopped. The 5th Division was part of the spearhead to reach the Rhine River and the Division began crossing the Rhine late on March 22, 1945 and finished during the day of the 23rd.

Tom thought the crossing of the Rhine was well organized. The boats arrived by truck and Tom helped unload them. Normally three men were assigned to a boat for river crossings, but only two were used at the Rhine. They were to take a load over, then push the boat out in the river and wait until a boat load of Engineers accumulated, then return. The Officers told them the reason for pushing the boats out in the river was to keep them from jamming up the crossing site. Tom thinks it may have been to keep everyone across. Tom and his partner kept their boat and went back immediately. Tom and his squad were then sent north to help with other crossings. The Navy was at the next place and had motorboats. The Navy did not like being there, but worked hard and did a good job. The crossing of the Rhine for the 5th Division was not really difficult. Most thought the Germans would vigorously defend the Rhine. They may have not been ready as the 3rd Army had moved fast to the crossing site.

The 5th Division moved over to the Autobahn and proceeded to Frankfurt clearing the way and taking prisoners. This was about April 1st and it was apparent the war was nearing the end. The 5th went to help clear the Rhur Valley, a large industrial area in Germany. Tom saw the first of many Concentration Camps in this area. He helped to set up water purification systems for the camps and the Medic's were busy checking and treating those who had been imprisoned by the Germans during the war. They left the gate open on one camp, but the prisoners raised such a ruckus with the local citizens they had to round them up and close the gates. They were given food and medical treatment. Tom told me that in recent research it has been proven that the Germans had as many as 20,000 of these camps. The German people have often denied they knew about them. This does not seem possible; they simply had to know they existed.

After helping to clear the Rhur Valley, the 5th Division made a quick move to Czechoslovakia. The war came to an end and Corporal Thomas B. Tucker returned to the States and was discharged from the Army at Fort Knox, Kentucky in October 1945. In 1946, Tom received the La Croix de Guerre 1940 Avec Palm from the Belgium Government.

After the war Tom worked as an Architectural Draftsman for ten years and became a licensed Architect in 1955. In 1957 he formed his own architectural firm and for over forty six years until retiring in 2003 helped to grow the firm into one of the leading firms in the San Diego area. His professional achievements include induction into the American Institute of Architects College of Fellows in 1982, and receiving an award from the city of Escondido for over thirty years of dedicated city planning community service.

Tom is an active member of the Society of the 5th Division and was selected by the society as "Man of the Year" in 2002 for his efforts to track down division World War II Missing in Action in France and to locate members of the 5th Division from the Vietnam War era.

On May 16, 2009 Tom was awarded the French Legion of Honor Medal. The Medal is open to all ranks and professions, either French citizens or foreign nationals and is conferred upon men and women for outstanding achievements in military or civilian life. The award is France's highest award.

5

D-DAY

The plan for invading France in Normandy had been discussed several times by the British and Americans. They could not agree about a cross channel invasion. The British remembered the loss of their forces when they were in France early in the war trying to help France in the fight with the invading German army. The German army had overrun France in a matter of days and pushed the British army to Dunkirk, Belgium. Dunkirk is along the coast across from England. The British lost large amounts of equipment and men. Winston Churchill feared another Dunkirk and thought the Normandy coast would run red with blood of British and American youth. Churchill was for a less aggressive approach to the invasion of France. The Americans had proposed a cross channel invasion in 1943, but the British thought they were not ready. Hindsight reveals that they were correct as the Americans soon learned in the fighting in North Africa.

Operation Torch was planned in early 1942. The Americans along with British forces would invade North Africa on November 8, 1942. Field Marshall Erwin Rommel was in command of the German army in North Africa. He was an excellent commander of the tank and infantry in fast moving battles. General George Patton Jr. was selected to command the American invasion force. It soon became evident that more training was needed for the Americans and they suffered a great loss at Kasserine Pass against Rommel's army. The American losses were 3,000 wounded and killed with 3,700 captured. The lesson learned would later pay dividends all through the war.

The planning for the invasion of the French coast at Normandy had been going on in England for many months.

The plans were being developed under the command of General Dwight D. Eisenhower, who would command all the Allied armies in Europe. He was aided by General Bernard Montgomery, the British top Field Commander.

A lot of questions had to be answered. How many Infantry, Artillery, Armored and Medical units would be necessary? They would also need ships of all sizes and landing craft to transport the men and equipment. Enormous amounts of equipment, food, medical supplies and later replacements had to be taken into account. A harbor for unloading the material was a must and plans were developed to build artificial harbors in England. The harbor would be towed across the channel and put in place after the landings. The harbor supporting the Americans was located at Utah beach and the British and Canadians harbor was on Gold beach near Arromanches. There would be problems involved in putting the pieces together and they could become separated during the channel crossing. The harbors were labeled Mulberry A for the Americans and Mulberry B for the British and Canadians. The Mulberry harbors worked well until a storm hit the Normandy coast on June 19 and lasted four days. They were repaired and used, but not to the extent originally planned. The harbor at Arromanches received less damage and was used until the middle of September. After September the Allies had capture ports along the French and Belgium coast and they were heavily used. A scale model of a Mulberry harbor can be seen in the Arromanches Museum.

Infantry Divisions required 400 tons of supplies per day, but Armored Divisions needed 1200 tons per day. Minimum requirements for the landing force were between 8,000 and 12, 000 tons per day. As more Divisions became involved in the fighting, the amounts became enormous.

Some ingenious instruments of war were devised for the invasion. British General Percy Hobart designed those used by the British army. The Americans called them, "Hobart's Funnies," and did not see a need for them. The Crab was a tank with a cylinder mounted on the front, extended out with pieces of chain. The cylinder was made to rotate causing the chain to hit the ground and set off land mines. The tank was heavy and did not perform well. Another was a thirty foot long bridge, folded in half, also mounted on a tank. The idea was to bridge across tank traps, small streams or as an aid in landing on the beach. The Americans fitted the Sherman tank with canvas skirts and propellers. The skirt could be raised around the tank causing it to float and the propellers would move the tank across the water to the beaches. Some of the tanks made it to the beach, but many were swamped by the high waves in the channel. In recent years divers have found the tanks off the Normandy coast.

The invasion at Normandy was the largest Amphibious Assault in history and probably will be the last of such proportion. The men working on the plan were determined to get it right. Many details had to be worked out and disagreements about how to accomplish the landing cropped up all the time. In the end all felt they had done everything possible to make the invasion a success. One of the major decisions was the date for the invasion. Favorable tide was available on only a few days. It was decided June 5, 1944 would be the day and everyone worked toward making it a reality. Ships had to be docked and made ready for loading; men and equipment were transported from all over England to the loading dock. The entire operation needed to be as secret as possible. Those who knew of the invasion date were almost imprisoned with confinement. A few talked publicly about the date and were severely punished.

The loading of ships began on June 3rd. On the 4th high wind and rain pounded England and the Normandy coast. High waves in the channel made crossing impossible and operations had to be postponed. The weather forecast for the 5th and 6th was for improved conditions and General Eisenhower gave the order to go. The storm left the channel with high waves and conditions on the ships were not good. The men were seasick and I am sure fear of the unknown was cause for some of the sickness.

Had you been on the bluffs behind Utah and Omaha beach when it began to get light on morning of June 6th the sight would have been overwhelming. The channel was full of ships of all sizes and numbered more than 2,700. They also had 2,600

Higgins Boats to take the men ashore. The only way to see all the ships was to fly over the channel. The 82nd and 101st Airborne Divisions saw the ships as they flew over on the way to their assigned drop zones. They later said, "With such a large invasion force, the enemy did not stand a chance." It looked as if one could walk across the channel stepping from one ship to another.

Because of the weather the Germans did not expect the invasion and their officers had gone to a map exercise. General Rommel, who was in command in Normandy, was also home for his wife's birthday. Hitler believed the invasion would occur at the Pas-de-Calais, the place that was the shortest distance across the channel from England to France. He had ordered several tank units to be held in the Pas-de-Calais and they were not to be assigned anywhere else without his approval.

During the planning the British and Americans had worked hard to convince the Germans they were going to invade at the Pas-de-Calais. They maintained fake radio transmission, designed to make the Germans believe they were coming soon.

Omaha Beach, calm and peaceful on this day in July 1998. Courtesy of the author.

A movie production company had made fake tanks, trucks, and large guns, knowing the Germans were doing photo reconnaissance. They worked hard on the deception and it worked. Hitler continued to believe the Normandy invasion was a fake and would not release the tanks. By the time Hitler was convinced, a lot of time had been lost. This did not mean the invasion was easy for the Allies, the Americans, British and Canadians.

The planning was finished, the troops and equipment were loaded and the invasion force was on its way across the channel. The storm had stopped as forecast. June 6, 1944 was D-Day, a day that will stand out in our history and be long remembered. Shortly after daylight bombing by the Allied Air Corps began on the beaches. Damage of the gun emplacements, pillboxes, and defense obstacles was minimal. The bombs almost missed the beach and the bluffs because the Air Corps did not want to short drop on the ships in the channel. The bombing was followed by shelling from the ships in the channel and they too did little damage. The troops were scheduled to come ashore at 0630. The Americans would land on Utah and Omaha and the British and Canadians on Gold, Juno and Sword. At the end of the day, 175,000 troops had come ashore and casualties were about 5,000 and half of them would be on Omaha.

The morning of the invasion, breakfast for the Americans was Spam sandwiches and coffee and the British and Canadians had fried eggs with a tot of rum. The troops began loading on the Higgins boats. The men carrying packs weighting sixty to eighty pounds made the climb down the nets to the boats difficult. The high waves caused the boats to bob up and down, making it hard to judge when to jump from the net. Some troops fell in the water and others received broken legs and other injuries. After each boat was loaded they circled until it was time to head for the shore and eleven months of hard fighting.

During my visit to Europe in 1998, we crossed the English Channel on a boat. The weather conditions that day would make it an exciting trip. We loaded on the tour bus in the morning for the drive to the coast. Our destination was a spot near Dover, across the channel from Calais. It was raining as we left our hotel in London. Our route took us through some old parts of London, then out to smaller villages, past Kent and Westerham, near Chartwell, Winston Churchill's home for forty years. The home is a National Trust property and maintained to preserve the look of Churchill's day. On arriving at our destination it was quickly apparent the high winds would cause the crossing to be a rough ride.

We made the crossing on a Hovercraft, a large boat with space for vehicles in the bottom and perhaps 400 passengers. The boat had a snack bar and restrooms, plus an observation deck, which no one would use on this trip.

After boarding we got a sandwich and drink. Soon after we started, it was apparent the ride was not going to be smooth. Two of my sisters and their husbands were touring with my wife and me. One of my brothers-in-law tried to go to the observation deck, but found it was impossible to stand and walk. He returned to his seat and soon reached for a barf bag. He lost his lunch, but recovered quickly and was all right for the rest of the trip. The boat was about half full and most of the people were seasick. The crew was passing out more barf bags and the restrooms were overflowing. The rough ride did not bother some as one young couple seemed to be sleeping. I did not get seasick.

We had a rough ride, but it was nothing like the men of the invasion force experienced. We were inside, in seats with armrest, warm and dry and not carrying packs weighing sixty to eighty pounds. At the end we would not be assaulting a beach involved in a desperate struggle. We were told the crossing was almost canceled because of the high winds and waves. The English Channel is often a rough ride and it was not smooth for the invasion force on June 6, 1944.

On Utah Beach the first wave was to land at 0630, with the second in their wake. The third wave was scheduled for 0645. None of the schedule was on time. All were off target by at least one mile, tides, winds, waves and too much screening smoke caused confusion. There were losses to floating mines and direct hits by the shore guns. Some of the Navy coxswain lost their nerve and unloaded men in waist deep water 200 to 300 yards from the shore. The ramps of the Higgins boats were dropped to unload the men and they became excellent targets for the German machine guns. Most of the men lost the breakfast of Spam sandwiches and were exhausted from all the confusion.

Brigadier General Theodore Roosevelt Jr., the 4th Division's Assistant Commander, and son of President Theodore Roosevelt was in the first wave to land on Utah Beach. He was a veteran of World War I, was fifty seven years old, the oldest American and only General Officer with the first wave. He realized they were off target, but was ashore and decided to start the war from the spot in which they landed. He walked up and down the beach giving directions, causing a big lift to the morale of the soldiers around him. His attitude was, "The men would think if a General came ashore with the first wave, it must not be all that bad." His leadership on D-Day earned him the Medal of Honor and command of the 90th Infantry Division. Sadly he died from a heart attack on July 12, 1944 and is buried in the American Cemetery behind Omaha Beach.

Omaha Beach was an obvious landing site. The sand was firm and the beach was ten kilometers long at low tide, with a stretch of sand 300 to 400 meters from shore to waterline. In 1944 a seawall existed that was part wood and masonry, one to four meters high. It is gone now. The bluff behind the seawall was steep. Vehicles could not climb the bluff, but a man could. Track and wheeled vehicles could exit the beach through one of five draws or ravines. The exit at Vierville was paved, the others ranged from a foot path to dirt roads. The Germans knew Omaha was a good landing site and had it well defended. Twelve strong points had the big guns, 88's and 75's and there were plenty of mortars along with dozens of machine guns. All guns were in concrete bunkers or pill boxes constructed of thick reinforced concrete. The guns had all been presighted to cover any possible angle.

Pointe- du- Hoc is located between Utah and Omaha beach and is a high point along the bluff. Men of the 5th Ranger Battalion climbed the rock walls using ropes. Several bunkers were on Pointe-du-Hoc and today one can see their location. The bombing or shelling by the Navy must have hit them as large slabs of concrete lay about, left in place after the war.

Members of the 116th Regiment of the 29th Infantry Division were told bombing would flatten everything on the beach and disable the guns on the bluff. The fighting would begin at the top of the bluff behind the beach. Few bombs fell on the beach and not many on the bluff. The bombers were late and missed vital targets; the shelling by the Navy was inaccurate and too brief to cause any great damage. The men at Omaha Beach experienced the same as at Utah. Landings were made at the wrong place and units were out of sequence. The Higgins boats had to battle high waves four to six feet high causing water to wash over the sides. The men bailed with helmets to help the pumps keep up and were exhausted on reaching the shore. Men let off the boats in deep water drowned because of the heavy packs, it was impossible to swim or stay afloat under the weight. Officer's and NCO's urged the men to get off the beach as it was evident they would be killed if they did not move up the bluff and inland.

I went to Normandy when visiting Europe in 1998 and to all the invasion beaches. It was afternoon when we came to Omaha Beach. Our tour bus came to the beach down Exit 1, from Vierville. The tide was out exposing 300 meters of the beach, the day was partly cloudy which is normal. I got off the bus and walked out on the beach looking at a calm channel, different than on June 6, 1944. I tried to imagine the channel filled with ships as it had been fifty four years earlier. I wondered what it was like to ride in a Higgins boat with six foot waves.

I turned and looked back at the bluff and noticed about half way up on my left an old gun that had fired on the men coming ashore on D-Day. It was not one preserved as a museum piece, but a rusting hunk of steel. The barrel was pointing up; I wanted to go turn it down. It seemed to still be in defiance of those who conquered the evil it once represented and I was angry about such a display. The bluff was what seemed to be too far for any to have survived the gun fire. The seawall is no longer there and I could not find any protection along the beach if guns were to fire at me. Chills ran up my back as I remembered those killed on D-Day. The cemetery behind Omaha is the final resting place for several thousand killed in Normandy.

None of the landings were easy. There were casualties at all the landing beaches. A lot of heroes were present that day, most not recognized with a medal. Junior Officers and NCO's led the determined men off the beach and up the bluff after they realized that to stay on the beach was to die. Most of the men in World War II were not professional soldiers, they were there as volunteers or draftees and would do their best to help win the war. They all wanted the same thing, to get the war over and return home to girlfriends, wives and family members. Of the eleven million soldiers in Europe, only one and one half million would be engaged in actual combat. Few got a rotation back to the states for a visit with family. They simply endured, wishing and praying the war would end soon.

6

NORMANDY

The 5th Division had spent eight months training for combat in Northern Ireland; on July 2, 1944 they began preparations to move to Normandy. The vehicles and equipment were the first to be loaded, followed by the troops and all began moving July 4th and 5th. The troops and equipment were on the way July 6th, their destination no longer a secret. All the ships dropped anchor on the evening of July 8th off the coast at Les Dunes de Vereville, France. The view of Utah Beach was unforgettable. They all could see half submerged, sunken and damaged ships, Pill boxes where the guns had been and silver barrage balloons rising in the sky. Grave Registration Units were collecting the dead, both American and enemy. The front may have been about four miles inland.

At 0600 the next morning, with a fine mist in the air, the 10th Regiment climbed down the cargo nets to the landing craft that would take them ashore. They were dressed in full combat gear, ready to engage the enemy if necessary. The Regiment unloaded from the landing craft on a pier made of sunken steel drums belted together. After reaching the beach, they left their gear for trucks to bring later. They marched from the beach to the town of Montebourg, a distance of eighteen miles. The men were wearing uniforms impregnated with a chemical that made the material stiff and would not let air through. The chemical was protection against gas attacks, such as the German Army used in World War I. They also carried gas mask that were bulky and made movement difficult. Most threw the mask away after a short time. They did not need them as the Germans did not use gas in the war. Many wore the impregnated uniforms for several weeks. If time permitted they boiled them in water to remove the chemical. Lt. Ralph Cupelli said, "They were so stiff, they would stand alone."

On the morning of July 14th, the 10th moved to relieve the 18th Regiment of the 1st Infantry Division in the area of Sallen, France. The move took them through St. Mere Eglise, Carentan and Isigny. These towns had seen heavy fighting by the 82nd and 101st Airborne Divisions early on D-Day. Their mission was to capture and hold the bridges for the Infantry coming ashore later in the day. Damage from bombs and artillery was everywhere; buildings and trees leveled. Dead cows and horses lay scattered over the pastures and fields. The Engineers were working with bulldozers to clear the area and fill in the holes.

As the 10th neared the front, German Artillery began shelling them, slowing their progress, but they were able to be in place shortly after dark in positions they occupied until the 23rd. They slowly began to learn the facts of war, how to recognize incoming and outgoing artillery, the need to be alert at all times. New Units went through a breaking in period which was called the, Baptism of Fire, and they would benefit from it for the rest of the war.

Lt. Bud Liebner said, "Shortly after they arrived in Normandy, Officers of the 10th were sent to observe the 1st In-

Men of the 10th Regiment in Normandy. Courtesy of Combat Narrative of the 10th Regt. in WW2.

fantry Division and I soon learned that we were very green at this business of war." The 1st Division was veterans of fighting in Africa and Sicily in 1943. He learned more from them than any school available at the time.

While in Normandy, a sniper, shooting from a tree almost killed Lt. Liebner. The bullet hit the ground at his feet and he could not believe the sniper missed. He carried a Thompson Machine Gun with a twenty round clip. He thinks he fired all twenty rounds and killed the sniper. There were lots of snipers in Normandy. They had constructed runways in the trees and could quickly move around to locate a target. They used rifles with scopes and rarely missed. Lt. Liebner was not as lucky on July 23rd as he led a patrol and received his first wound of the war. All but one of the patrol was wounded or killed.

Lt. Harold Storey arrived in Normandy and was assigned to the 10th Regiment along with seventy two others on July 25th. He replaced Lt. Liebner as Platoon Leader of the 2nd Platoon of C Company.

The Allies became stuck in Normandy; they had not been able to push the German Army out. Part of the problem was the hedgerows. The hedgerows provided good defensive positions for the Germans. The hedge had been growing for years and was tall and thick. The farmers had let the hedge be a fence between the fields. There were openings for farmers to enter and work the land. The hedge covered the roads like a tunnel. The Germans had placed guns in strategic positions and could fire on any soldier entering the space. Tanks were of little use in the hedge, until a Sergeant thought of using the steel beach obstacles to fashion a cutter. The Engineers were busy for several days making and wielding the cutter to the front of the tanks. The tanks would make a run at the hedge and cut at least part way through and then explosives were used to widen the space for tanks and Infantrymen. These tanks were named, "Rhinos, "and were an effective and deciding factor in the Normandy Campaign.

Soldiers did not have much privacy during the war and use of the latrine was one example. The latrines were a slit trench, several feet long and no screen was provided. They of course were necessary, but were placed out in the open, often in the back part of a garden. Sanitation required them to be covered when a unit moved on. Signs were posted saying, "Old Latrine-July 25, 1944". Language was a problem between the Americans and the French and the French on seeing the old latrine would mistake them for graves and flowers were often placed on them.

Booby traps were a part of war and the Germans used them in Normandy in several ways. They cut trees felling them across roads and then placed explosives in them, making it difficult for wheeled vehicles to move. The hidden explosives made it dangerous for armored vehicles to clear the road. Land mines were then placed in the path of obvious detours. Soldiers were always looking for souvenirs and the Germans took advantage of this desire by putting grenades under dead soldiers and the souvenir hunter could be killed or wounded when searching for something to take home after the war.

General Omar Bradley, Commander of the 1st Army in Normandy, devised a plan to breakout of the hedge row country. He named it, "Cobra." The plan was to bomb an area around St. Lo and break the German line which held the Allies in Normandy. For more than two hours 3,000 bombers attacked the area. The 10th Regiment, near Foret de Cerisy was not part of the attack to follow the bombing, but was close enough to see the bombs falling. Smoke and dust soon obscured the target and the later planes missed the target and bombs fell on some American units, killing and wounding them. In spite of the confusion, some units were able to immediately attack. The plan worked and the breakout of Normandy picked up speed as the Americans began to move forward.

The 5th Division began attacking after the bombing on the 27th. The 10th Regiment was at hill 183 and involved in hard fighting with elements of the German 3rd and 5th Parachute Divisions. The Parachute Divisions were well trained and considered good soldiers. Hill 183 was part of the ring the Germans had along the beachhead. Battle designations were often named after a hill and had to do with the elevation. It was a tough fight, but the 10th prevailed.

The 3rd Army became active by the first of August and was commanded by General George S. Patton Jr. Gen. Patton was a capable commander with confidence in his ability as a leader and in the ability of the soldiers he led. The men of C Company have told me they liked and respected him and thought he was a capable commander. Jack Davis said, "There is no question about it, we liked him." Ralph Cupelli and Bud Liebner echoed his words. Divisions to be assigned to the 3rd Army had been waiting in England and Northern Ireland, but were now in Normandy. The 5th Division was the second unit to be assigned and would remain with the 3rd Army for the entire war.

The first day Lt. Harold Storey was leader of the second Platoon, he thought he had been wounded when a grenade was thrown over a hedgerow. When the grenade exploded it broke a limb from the hedge and a piece hit Lt. Storey causing only a large bruise. He quickly wondered what he would say to his father if he had really been wounded in his butt.

Uncle Wallace wrote his mother on July 12, telling her he was in France and again on the 25th saying the weather had been nice. He could not write about the weather while training in Northern Ireland. The other letters in July do not mention anything about combat. I am sure any comment about combat would have been censored. A letter dated July 29th explains that he has been busy and does not have much time to write.

On August 4th, the 10th moved toward LaTrinte and again saw tremendous battle damage. Their route took them through St. Lo, which had been reduced to rubble from the bombing, then on through St. Georges-de-Reintembault toward Avranches and out into open country away from the hedgerows. They then went through Fougeres and country that had not been affected by the war. The French people greeted them with open arms offering fruit, wine, and all kinds of food. Lt. Storey remembers one day a man and his two daughters approached them offering a drink from a bottle of clear liquid. He had small glasses, about one third ounce. He allowed the men to drink a small amount and they all made a face at the taste. They insisted he have some also. He said, "It burned all the way to my stomach." It was Calvados, an apple brandy and was probably home brewed. The soldiers were always alert when given drinks for fear of being poisoned. They did not at this time know who to trust. The next day Lt. Storey received word to report to his Company Commander, Captain Davis. He was reprimanded for drinking with his men, a serious case of fraternization. It was the only reprimand he received during his time in combat.

Next was Vitre, a beautiful city. The people were seeing a column of Army vehicles and soldiers in olive drab and they were the closest thing to war that had been in their town. The 5th Division was moving fast in an attempt to keep the Germans moving and not have time to build a defensive line. Lt. Storey remarked, "We were almost like shock troops." They did not get time for sleep or hot meals. They went to Angers and crossed the Main River making contact with the enemy, but had few loses. The 5th Division moved on through St. Calais and again the troops were cheered by the local people as they went through the town.

The Division was preparing to take Chartres on August 13th. The 3rd Platoon led by Lt. Ralph Cupelli, of C Company of the 1st Battalion along with help from a Tank Destroyer Unit captured a German Quartermaster Warehouse that held stores of food, clothing and liquor. Lt. Cupelli's Platoon was ordered to guard the warehouses, which turned out to be a difficult assignment that got him in trouble. Soon all of the 5th Division learned of the captured warehouse and the goodies it held. Trucks began arriving from each of the units demanding their share of the loot. Lt. Cupelli was out ranked by officers from the units and they took wine and liquor and other items. Colonel Bell, Commander of the 10th Regiment took cans of tuna and tomato paste for the kitchen to use, which probably improved the quality of meals for a time. Col. Bell liked to drink and when he ask for his favorite liquor, was told it was all gone, he became angry and ordered Lt. Cupelli put under arrest. The charge was looting. Lt. Cupelli reported to his commander Capt. Davis and was shown the list of charges. Nothing came of the incident and Lt. Cupelli believes the Executive Officer of the Regiment, Lt. Col. Breckenridge was responsible for convincing Col. Bell to drop the charges. Lt. Cupelli could have spent years in jail had he been convicted. Lt. Cupelli remembers men from his 3rd squad found some eggs and bacon and after locating a stove and cooking pans, enjoyed a great feast. If each of us has fifteen minutes of fame in our lives, Ralph thinks the arrest at Chartres may have been his fifteen minutes.

During the fight for Chartres, the division destroyed fifty planes, German ME109's at the airport. They also secured the release of fifty American prisoners and captured 922 Germans. Tanks, trucks and large guns were also part of the take, reducing the German army's ability to fight.

One of the major battles of Normandy was occurring around Falaise. The Americans from the south and the British and Canadians from the north had the opportunity to surround the remainder of the German Army in Normandy in a pincer movement. The estimate was that approximately 200,000 men could have been captured. Estimates are that about 50,000 managed to escape. They failed in the attempt because of fear of firing on each other while forming the circle. Actions by both have been the subject of controversy since the war. The German Army was retreating, taking all men and equipment from Normandy and they were perfect targets for fighter planes and dive bombers. In spite of the mechanization during World War II, the Germans were using horses to pull wagons of ammunition and some big guns. After the battle was over the roads were littered with destruction and had to be cleared using bulldozers. The odor from dead horses and humans was horrendous and Fighter Pilots reported the smell was bad from a few hundred feet above.

The Allies had several hundred thousand troops in Normandy along with tanks, tank destroyers, artillery units, and wheeled vehicles of all sizes. They also had control of the air with planes operating at will looking for targets of opportunity. The troops fighting in Normandy were now veterans. They had received their baptism of fire and more. The emphasis was on speed, keep the enemy moving and they would not have time to form a defensive line. The 5th Division had become good at fighting and living while moving fast. The soldiers rode on anything mobile. There were eight or ten on a medium tank, twelve or fourteen on a tank destroyer and four or five in each Jeep. They went through sun, rain, mud, dust and flowers and had plenty of cognac and calvados. Pfc. Jack Davis got drunk in Normandy and slept through an air attack. He never did that again during the war.

7

BATTLE FOR METZ

After Chartres the 5th Division started going east to objectives that took them south of Paris to Etampes, Fontainebleau and Montereau. Etampes was taken on August 22nd. The 10th Regiment started the advance on Montereau on the 23rd. The FFI, French Forces of the Interior, were holding bridges for the Americans. Some bridges had been booby trapped with bombs and they had to be removed by the mine platoon of a tank company. As the Regiment moved toward Montereau they heard explosions in the town and knew the Germans had blown up some of the bridges. During the night of the 23rd they had to contend with a severe electrical storm and heavy rainfall. The advance continued on the 24th and Montereau was taken. In the days to follow, the 10th moved through several smaller towns and villages. The Regiment crossed the Seine River at St Nicolas where they had several wounded. The wounded were put on a boat, clearly marked with Red Crosses and as they were rowed back across for medical treatment; the Germans waited until the boat was near the middle of the river and opened fire, sinking the boat. The wounded could not swim and all were drowned. Killing of wounded was against the Geneva Convention Rules of War. The Germans had signed the charter, but often did not adhere to the rules.

A report in the 10th Regiment's 1st Battalion area on the 25th told of five German soldiers in some woods nearby. A six man patrol was formed to round them up. The patrol located the small band of soldiers and surrounded them. They put up their hands as if to surrender and as the patrol moved forward about thirty of their comrades fired with machine guns and rifles. Two men of the patrol were wounded and the others pinned down for a time. The patrol was able to get back to their company and report. Maj. Haughey ordered tank destroyers to fire directly into the woods. The enemy was flushed out and many were killed as they tried to run away.

Epernay and Reims followed and the 10th was on battle fields of World War I. The war had been fought twenty five years earlier, but evidence of the fighting could be seen everywhere. Men in World War II had fathers in the fighting around Reims in World War I and now the sons were again at war with the Germans. Reims had warehouses full of Brandy, Champagne, cakes and fruit. I am sure the men of the 10th had the opportunity to sample some of the goodies.

The fighting continued on to Verdun and across the Meuse River by August 30th. The 10th Regiment was awarded the French Fourragere with Palm for taking the right bank of the river. The 5th Division was awarded the French Fourragere for the recapture of Verdun. The men of the 10th were now veterans; it had not been long since they walked on the sand of Utah Beach. They had moved 700 miles, crossed six rivers and taken 3,700 prisoners.

The speed of the 3rd Army was causing a problem with supplies. The 3rd had covered more distance than had been anticipated by the planners and they were out of gasoline and low on ammunition and food. The 3rd Army needed 400,000 gallons of gasoline per day for tanks and trucks. Supplies for the front were being delivered by a system called the Red Ball Express. The system needed 6,000 trucks and 23,000 men to keep them running twenty four hours per day. In spite of a great effort the system could not keep up. In eighty one days the Red Ball Express hauled more than 412,000 tons of ammunition, food, medical supplies, weapons and clothing and tried to keep the Divisions fighting.

Gasoline was finally delivered by planes, such as the B-24, a four engine heavy bomber. It was accomplished by loading five gallon cans of gas in the bomb bay of the planes and flying to temporary fields near Nancy. Ray Lemons a cousin of Uncle Wallace was a crew member on a B-24 and remembers making several trips to Nancy. He said, "These trips were not counted as combat missions." Uncle Wallace and Ray never met and would not have known they were cousins if they had been side by side in the work to deliver the gas.

The next objective of the 3rd Army was the crossing of the Moselle River near the French city of Metz. Metz, fortress city and capitol of Lorraine, had never been captured in its long history of war. The city was ringed by an inner and outer circle of twenty two forts and miscellaneous bunkers. The Forts were constructed of steel-reinforced concrete. They contained power plants, workshops, living quarters and gun emplacements, connected by a network of tunnels. Bombing by the Air Corps and constant shelling by Artillery did little damage.

Historians have called the battle for Metz and the crossing of the Moselle River, one of three major battles in World War II. The 5th, 80th and 90th Divisions were there from the start and were later joined by the 95th Division. After the 95th arrived, Joseph Goebbels, one of Hitler's War Ministers, told the people of Germany, the 95th was a combination of the 5th and 90th Divisions. He claimed the 5th and 90th had been decimated by the German Army and the two Divisions had been combined to form the 95th. This was a lie, as were most of the things he was telling the German people about the progress of the war.

The battle at Metz has been analyzed by Historians and also by the Advanced Infantry Officers Course at Fort Benning, Georgia. Hindsight gives them the advantage, which no member of the Planning Staff of the 3rd Army enjoyed in September, 1944. The conclusions of all are that not enough reconnaissance was done prior to the attack. The co-ordination of units was poorly done and the strength of the defenders was miscalculated.

After their losses in Normandy, the Germans had been retreating fast and it was thought they were going back to the German border and behind the Siegfried Line, or more commonly called the West Wall. The 3rd Army had been moving fast, without much resistance and badly miscalculated the strategy of Hitler and his Generals. The German defense at Metz became a three month long battle for the 3rd Army with a large number of casualties.

After being resupplied the 3rd Army was ready for the assault on Metz. The first attempt was made by the 11th Regiment of the 5th Division on September 7th. The 2nd Regiment provided support for the 11th Regiment as they forced a bridgehead at Dornot. The crossing was difficult and the 11th had severe casualties, but did manage to cross the river and form a bridgehead, but could not enlarge the area. Heavy enemy counterattacks and the fact that no tanks could be brought across the river contributed to the 11th Regiments failure to maintain the attack. The 11th was withdrawn and new plans were made.

The 10th Regiment was given orders to cross at Arnaville, about two miles south of Dornot. The river was about one hundred yards wide at Arnaville and the banks were suitable for launching assault boats. Each man in the 10th was loaded with ammunition, three K rations and a full canteen of water. They quietly carried the boats to the river and began crossing a few minutes after midnight on September 9th. A Company of the 1st Battalion crossed first followed by C Company and were not discovered until after they crossed. While C Company was waiting to cross, Capt. Davis called for Lt. Storey to come to him. Capt. Davis had not felt Lt. Storey had the training to be an effective Platoon Leader as he was a replacement officer in Normandy and had not trained with the company in Ireland. He told Lt. Storey this would be the toughest test they had faced in the war to this point and that he had chose the 2nd platoon to lead the assault for C Company as he felt they were the most likely to succeed. Lt. Storey was aware of the Captain's feelings and he believes he actually apologized for not having much faith in his ability in the beginning. Capt. Davis also explained how important the capture of Metz was to the 3rd Army. Across the river was a flat area about 500 yards wide and had to be crossed before any concealment was available. In the absence of Lt. Col. Frank Langfitt, who had been evacuated because of hepatitis, Maj. Wilfred Haughey was in command and realized they had to get off the flat ground quickly. He was correct as the Germans soon discovered the crossing and began heavy firing with artillery. Maj. Haughey ordered Lt. Harris, his S-3, to find a way up the hill. Lt. Harris took one platoon from A Company and one from C Company and quickly made his way up the hill. The enemy had discovered the crossing and the rest of A Company and C Company sustained heavy casualties going up the hill. C Company took out an 88mm gun and its crew before gaining the high ground. After crossing the river and gaining the high ground the 10th was to secure the hill north of the town of Arry.

Metz was the home of an Officers Candidate School and several classes had worked out a plan to defend Hill 386, the objective of the 10th. The plan had been demonstrated and worked out to perfection. The schools candidates were ready and waiting for the attack. All the guns in the forts had been presighted and they were ready for a fight.

The other Regiments of the 5th had been keeping the enemy occupied by firing across the river, reducing the German force that could be sent to Arnaville. The heaviest counterattack occurred at noon on September 10th. An enemy tank company, supported by infantry jumped off from behind the town of Arry and tried a double envelopment of the 1st Battalion. C Company took the brunt of the attack and their commander Capt. William Davis was wounded in both legs. His radio operator was killed and Capt. Davis strapped the radio on his

L-R, Maj. Wilfred Haughey, Lt Col. Frank Langfitt. Courtesy of Frank Langfitt.

back and for a short time, continued directing artillery fire and the placement of the company. Capt. Davis had to be evacuated for medical treatment and was placed on a litter. While being carried off the battlefield, he was again hit by shell fragments and was killed. Lt. Eugene Dille, Executive Officer of C Company, took command.

Companies I and K of the 3rd Battalion were sent to take the town of Arry. The enemy was concentrated in the town with tanks along the side streets. The two companies cleared the town and were then withdrawn. Later it was determined the town was again occupied and C Company was sent to clear the enemy once more. Reconnaissance reported the town did not have a heavy concentration of troops, but C Company ran into a tough fight. The 2nd Platoon, led by Lt. Harold Storey had been in the lead as the company went up Hill 386. It was not known how many had been killed or wounded during the assault and Lt. Dille placed the 2nd Platoon in the rear as C Company moved to Arry. When the company reached the gate and wall around Arry they received machinegun fire and realized the town was occupied.

Lt. Dille was killed and Lt. Ralph Cupelli was wounded, by the same gunner that shot Lt. Dille. Lt. Cupelli's Platoon Sergeant, Robert Johnson shot the enemy gunner. By this time C Company had lost about eighty percent of their members who were killed, wounded or captured.

After two days of fighting the company was down to two officers and forty two enlisted men of the 206 that had crossed the river and started up Hill 386. Lt. Storey was a replacement in Normandy and the other officer was his senior and should have taken command of the company, but he claimed he was sick and could not go on. The officer's attitude had been bad for some time and the other officers had avoided him, not wanting to hear talk about defeat and death. As a combat leader he was no longer effective and was assigned to other duties. The men of C Company never saw him again during the war.

Lt. Storey led the small group that was left of C Company back to Hill 386. They were placed in a patch of woods that was thought to be protected from enemy observation. They soon experienced firing from German Artillery. The enemy was monitoring the 3rd Army's radio messages and would fire on them simultaneously with the 3rd Army guns. Lt. Storey soon figured out they were being seen from Ft. Driant and that their own artillery was not misfiring. Lt. Storey asks the Battalion Commander for permission to move his men to another location where they could be useful and not setting ducks. Permission was granted and they moved to a gap by A Company.

The men of C Company dug in, two men to a foxhole, the rocky ground made digging hard work. They fought well causing many casualties for the enemy. Lt. Storey had placed two 30 caliber machine guns in an ideal spot and they did their work well. The group had four bazookas, but the fins on the shells had gotten bent and they were inaccurate, but still helped. Lt. Storey, because of intense pressure, slept little for the next 150 hours. The men took heavy shelling for about six days. Pfc. Robert Brown, a man with a great sense of humor and had kept the company going in difficult times was killed when a piece of shrapnel went through his helmet. Fighter planes reported seeing a large number of enemy casualties in front of C Company positions. Lt. Storey was awarded the Silver Star Medal for his action on Hill 386, but he believes the pilots may have inflated the number of casualties.

Uncle Wallace was part of the fight to cross the river and get up Hill 386, the attempt to enter Arry and the next six days of shelling. I am sure by this time he had become a very savvy combat soldier. In a letter written in September, not dated, he tells his mother, "I hope you are fine. I am not so good, I am so nervous I can hardly write." This is not surprising after what he had just gone through. This was the only letter he indicated he had been through a dangerous time in combat and I am sure there were others.

In a September 30th letter, Uncle Wallace writes about being on the front line for a long time and has not had time to write. He mentions wearing his clothes for about sixty days and can only imagine what he looks like, also that a man from Oklahoma joined his squad. I am sure this man was Phillip Clover and they were to become good friends. In late September, the 10th Regiment had received twelve officers and 420 enlisted men as replacements.

From the first day of combat on July 14th to October 21st, the 10th had lost 20 officers and 279 enlisted men killed. In addition, wounded accounted for 20 officers and 1,593 enlisted men. Along with Phillip Clover came John Chichilla, from Pennsylvania. Both men were passed thirty years of age and near the limit of age for the draft.

The weather had been good up to October, when it began to rain and turn cool. Foxholes filled up with water and were more like bath tubs and the mud made movement of vehicles and tanks impossible at times. Lt. Storey remembers, despite different ways of trying, he was never able to completely cover his entire body with a GI raincoat. Constantly wet boots and socks caused an epidemic of trench foot, resulting in casualties; a problem they were forbidden to write home about. The men could not find a place to dry out. They were told to change socks often and dry and massage the feet. The problem was where and when this could take place. Most tried to follow instructions by keeping one pair of socks in their helmet having a dry pair, while wearing the other. Foot problems were to occur all through the war. Cold, freezing weather was even worse than rain. The Infantry was moving on their feet constantly and the need for better foot wear was not completely solved until years after the war.

With the replacements came Officers to fill the vacancy of Company Commander and Platoon Leaders in C Company. A short time later and after many mistakes the new commander, along with two platoon leaders had to be replaced because it was evident they did not have the experience and training to be effective in an Infantry Company.

Lt Harold Storey was assigned the position of Company Commander, a job of great responsibility. Replacements had put the company at full strength, after almost eighty percent had been lost in the first few days of the battle to capture Metz. It must have been an immense task to train and reorganize C Company.

The 3rd Army was again short of supplies; gasoline was the big problem. At this time the infantry tried repeatedly to gain entry to the forts and could not gain much. They made entry into the tunnels and the engineer's placed charges against steel doors, but they did little damage. They next tried to cut through the doors with welding torches. The Germans placed charges at the doors and set them off as the Americans tried to enter; the cost was high in wounded and killed. Pfc. Jack Davis and Cpl. Tom Tucker have both said this was a most terrible time for them. The tunnels were described as a hell hole and their memory of the time there is still with them. The 10th was withdrawn and sent to a rest spot, north of Joppecourt, where they received showers, clean clothes, haircuts and hot food. I am sure Uncle Wallace looked different and felt better.

After the first of November, the 3rd Army was again resupplied and orders were given for the attack on Metz. Gen. Patton called a meeting of the Officers of the 10th. They were to meet on a hill, off a paved road. Lt. Storey noticed when he arrived that high ranking officers came in clean vehicles; all parked in military fashion, while the company officers came in mud splattered jeeps. After a short wait a jeep came down the highway going fast and up the muddy hill slinging mud. Gen. Patton climbed out wiping mud from his face. The General gave an impassioned speech, with expletives and tears as was his custom. He told them more men would be killed and wounded before Metz was taken.

At this time of the fighting Pfc. Jack Davis got involved in an incident that would earn him a nickname. Davis was going through an area where the 10th had many casualties both killed and wounded. Someone had put up a sign, PURPLEHEART LANE, and as he stopped to read it, noticed a beehive in a tree nearby. He always liked to have honey in his coffee and the army did not furnish such luxury. He said, "I thought I was probably going to be killed and I wanted some honey." Back home his family had bees and he knew how to harvest honey, but did not have a hood to keep the bees off. He went to the tree and got the hive and remembers being stung fourteen times, but had some honey for several days. His buddies ever after have called him, Beehive Jack. Despite the pain from the stings, he thinks it was worth the effort.

Lt. Storey describes C Company's entry into Metz as being the place he felt would get him. After the brutal fighting on Hill 386 and the attempt to enter the forts, it did not seem he could last another fight. C Company was ordered to a street on the east side of Metz. The company was by three small houses when they were fired on by 20mm antiaircraft guns wounding five men. They took cover in the houses, knowing they could not reach their objective by taking the route assigned. After talking to Battalion, by radio, and receiving permission to alter their course, Lt Storey left the wounded with a Medic and asks for volunteers to follow him across a muddy beet field. He told the men there would not be any protection until they reached the edge of town. He started across the muddy field and after a time realized all accept the wounded and the Medic was following him. It was a dangerous situation, but they were not seen and reached the houses on the edge of town. They then saw a German sentry, but for some reason he ignored them. He must have been sleepy and thought they were some of his own men.

 Lt. Storey thinks C Company may have been the first to reach the heart of the city. The German soldiers came out of their quarters and surrendered on seeing the Americans and C Company took about 400 prisoners before noon. Civilians speaking English gathered around the men. They had captured a German command car and gave it to some reporters, telling them to paint it or they would be a target for American guns. Lt. Storey was able to contact Battalion on his radio, talking to Capt Bob Todd, operations officer. Capt. Todd was a capable officer, but often used profanity, which Lt. Storey did not appreciate. Capt. Todd ask, "Where in the GD Hell are you, we thought you were all dead." Lt. Storey told him and asks for transportation for the 400 prisoners causing Capt. Todd to exclaim with more expletives.

 Lt. Storey was able to quarter his men in an apartment building for the next two days giving them the luxury of sleeping in a bed for at least two nights. The second day Lt. Storey was not feeling well, with flu like symptoms and asks a Medic to make a toddy in an attempt to get rid of his ailment. He did feel better the next morning after much sweating during the night. The next day at 0600 a runner came to Lt. Storey telling him they had been ordered to one of the Forts that were still holding out. The commander of the fort came out and was told to surrender or be subjected to bombing by American planes. The weather was bad and Lt. Storey said even the birds were walking, so the commander did not take seriously the bombing threat and went back and held out until they ran out of food. Within the next two days Metz was completely in American hands. The battle that started on September 7th was over November 21, 1944.

The Seille River flows into the Moselle in Metz and the Engineers set charges to blow a bridge over the Seille to force the Germans to stay out of Metz. As they were about to set off the charge a man in uniform was seen walking toward the bridge. Sgt. Warren Mullins yelled for him to stop, but the man kept going. Sgt. Mullins, thinking he was part of the enemy force and might be going to cut the wire on the charges shot him. Jack Davis along with others went out and brought him inside the apartment building. He had two bullet wounds, but was alive. They then learned he was a mailman for Metz and must have thought they were not yelling at him. The bridge blew up soon after Sgt. Mullins fired, saving the man's life. The man lived and Sgt. Mullins was relived his shots had not been fatal.

Pfc. Jack Davis remembers he and six others got cut off from the main group on November 15th. He was serving as a medic with B Company and they were attacking in the early morning through a wooded area. The enemy had placed snipers throughout the woods, but in the darkness neither could see the other. When it became lighter, they could see the enemy setting up a machine gun by some trees in the distance and were preparing a counterattack. One man was hit by a sniper and Pfc. Davis went to help him, knowing they were in trouble; he put a bandage on the man and told him to go back and get A Company to help. The man started back and Pfc. Davis returned to the fight and got behind a pile of wood. Another man, whom Pfc. Davis did not know was also there. He was armed with only a carbine, which was a 30 caliber rifle, but did not have the knockdown power of the standard M1 rifle carried by most infantrymen. Medics did not carry a rifle which was according to the Geneva Convention Rules of War. Pfc. Davis did carry a pistol in his pocket at times, but it was only for use in a hand to hand situation. The man took off running, leaving Pfc. Davis without any protection.

Pfc. Davis managed to get with some of his group and saw Lt. Hawthorne and a trooper named Cross with a machine gun set up on a tripod. They all knew they were in danger of being shot or captured. Cross took the machine gun, leaving the tripod; he carried the gun and began firing as they ran. Carrying a machine gun and firing it at the same time is difficult as the gun and belt of ammunition are heavy. A man running near them stumbled and almost fell. They grabbed him and helped get him out of the shelling. They noticed he had been shot through the neck, the shell going through not hitting a vital spot. Companies A and C had reached them at this time and the man was evacuated to a field hospital.

When C Company later entered Metz, they found a German Hospital with wounded Americans. A soldier who had seen all of the shooting told them Pfc. Davis had been killed because no one could survive that much shelling and be alive. When A Company heard what the man said, they teased Pfc. Davis, telling him, "Jack that was A Company shooting at you."

Pfc. Davis remembers a man in his group was always complaining. The weather was bad, the food was not good and if they had done things differently, all would be better. He could not find anything good to talk about. One day in a battle and the chips were down, the man laid down a barrage of rifle fire and fought well. They could not believe he was capable of doing such a thing. His action that day made him the topic of conversation for some time.

In October, Uncle Wallace wrote telling his mother, "Write often, I feel better when I get lots of mail." He also talks about the babies his sisters have had remarking, "I will have some new kin folks to see when I get home." In November his letters are about Franklin Roosevelt being re-elected and has decided he will not be home for Christmas this year, but does not think the war will last much longer.

Many of the top Brass of the army was talking about the war being over by Christmas. This attitude may be the reason they became lax and were not prepared for Hitler's surprise attack in the Ardennes Forest in Belgium on December 16th.

8

BATTLE OF THE BULGE

On November 30th, the 10th Regiment, attached to the 95th Division was ordered to the Saar Basin along the German border. They were close to the small town of Kreutzwald, near Saarbrucken. They spent the first few days clearing the small towns in the area and cleared Ludweiler on December 9th. They encountered more snipers here than at any other place during the war.

The rest of the 5th Division arrived and the 10th was again home with the other Regiments of the 5th. From the 9th to the 19th the Division was in reserve, receiving replacements and training for the attack on the Siegfried Line, or the West Wall. The West Wall was built by the Germans to protect them from invasion through France, Luxembourg and the Netherlands. The fortification consisted of two belts about one mile apart. Concrete pyramids about three feet high, referred to as Dragons Teeth, ran for miles along the border. Trenches were dug on one side of the pyramids and were about ten to twelve feet deep designed to keep tanks from crossing. Pillboxes with all sizes of guns with interlocking fire were put all along the border. The Atlantic Wall was for protection from amphibious assault in Normandy and then the West Wall was built to further protect them. The Allies were to have some difficult battles before finally penetrating the West Wall, but were able to overcome the German resistance.

Lt. Storey remembers C Company was promised hot food one evening. They were near the German border in rough terrain with rain most of the day. The food was delivered by Jeep pulling a small trailer. About 2030 hours that evening, the Jeep driver, T/5 Stallbaum appeared, shook up, out of breath and began apologizing. The Jeep and trailer had slide off the muddy road and were so far down in a ravine it could not be recovered. The driver had been observing blackout conditions and could not see. Lt. Storey understood how such a thing could happen and told him, "Don't worry, they had plenty of K rations and no one would go hungry." I have wondered if the Jeep and trailer with the marmite cans containing C Company's meal are still in the ravine today. In the uninhabited areas of Europe, lots of war equipment can be found, more than sixty years later.

On the Jeep was a toy siren that T/5 Stallbaum had taken from another vehicle. Lt. Storey had ridden in the Jeep and pulled the cord sounding the siren a few times. It made a lot of noise and was frowned on by the Brass. Lt. Storey said, "As a footslogger they got pushed around and it was fun to do a little payback."

The 5th Division was in position on December 20th for their attack on the West Wall. Lt. Storey remembers being told by higher command of a breakthrough by the Germans in the north, but they did not know many details. The 5th Division was about to be engaged in the largest battle ever fought by the American Army. The battle would have different names, but most remember it as the Battle of the Bulge or the Ardennes Offensive. It began with the German attack in the early morning hours on December 16, 1944.

After action reports have been reviewed since the war and the conclusion is high command did not pay attention to reports of a possible build up by the German Army in the Ardennes Forrest in Northern Belgium. They all had been thinking the Germans were about to surrender and the war would soon be over. The Allies had pushed the Germans out of Normandy and Northern France. Most of Belgium and the Netherlands had also been cleared. The Allies held a line from the Netherlands, through Belgium and France and were close to the German border, not far from the Rhine River, thought to be the place of the Germans last effort to win the war. The Germans had also been fighting a two front war, the Americans, British, Canadians, some French forces and units from other small countries on the west and the Russians on the east.

The Germans were being squeezed in and could not possibly win the war.

Hitler and the German high command had been planning an attack for the past four months. The Germans had great success early in the war, with an attack through the Ardennes Forrest in Belgium and Luxembourg. They had overrun both countries in a matter of weeks and Hitler believed it could happen again. If the plan worked, they would split the Allied Armies, then cross the Meuse River and capture the ports at Antwerp, Belgium, through which supplies flowed for the Allies. Hitler also believed it would cause confusion in the Allied Command and they would have to go to their respective governments for new orders. The Allies did not work in such manner; the Allied Commander had the authority to make adjustments and did not have to wait on the governments to make a decision. Hitler knew the weather in that part of Europe during December and January was usually cloudy, foggy or snowing, which would keep the Allied Air Corps grounded. His tanks could move about and not be worried about air attacks.

The Germans had amassed large amounts of equipment and troops in the Ardennes. Movement of troops and equipment had been at night and they were put in hiding, making it hard for planes on reconnaissance to see them. Hitler had ordered no radio transmissions concerning the build up. The Field Generals responsible for implementing the plan shook their heads and knew immediately the plan would not work as the Allies had the man power and equipment to stop the attack quickly. They all felt it was too ambitious and would not result in Germany gaining the advantage. Hitler paid no attention to his Field Generals and the attack began early in the morning on December 16, 1944.

In early December new Division arriving in Europe were sent to what was considered a quiet section of the line in northern Belgium. None had been through their baptism of fire and were green troops. The German attack hit the 106th Infantry Division and they were quickly overwhelmed. The 106th took severe casualties and complete Companies were captured. The attack was vicious and not expected. Divisions with combat experience were hit hard and they were soon disorganized and men were scattered, some were running or going back by any vehicle available. Small groups were organized by NCO's and Junior Officers, setting up roadblocks to stop or slow the advance of the enemy. The surprise attack caused confusion for the Americans, but General Officers quickly began to reorganize the divisions.

When Gen. Eisenhower received reports of the attack, he looked at his map and ordered the 82nd and 101st Airborne Divisions into action. The Airborne was trained to fight in difficult situations and this was a job for them. Both divisions had been resting and receiving replacements in France. They had come from the failed attack in the Netherlands, known as Market-Garden, planned by British General B.L. Montgomery. They had been badly mauled trying to help the British forces cross the Rhine River at Arnhem. Before the Divisions were rested, re-equipped and ready, they were loaded on trucks and rushed, at night, with headlights on, to Belgium to stop the German attack. The 101st along with pieces of units broken up by the attack were soon surrounded in Bastogne, Belgium.

The 3rd Army G-2, Colonel Oscar Koch, had been keeping an eye on a build up of panzer and infantry units and dumps of ammunition and gasoline west of the Rhine River. Rail movement was on the increase and there had not been any radio transmission concerning the build up. He was concerned and reported his findings to Gen. Patton. After the early morning attack on December 16th, Gen. Patton called a meeting of the 3rd Army staff and told them, "We will be asked to go save their hides." The staff made three action plans to move the 3rd Army if the need arose. Generals Eisenhower, Patton, Bradley and others met in Verdun to decide how to handle the situation. Gen. Patton told "Ike" about his plan and that he could counterattack in Luxembourg with three divisions. The other Army Commanders present did not have plans or solutions to correct the current situation.

The 5th Division received orders to withdraw from their attack on the West Wall, when relieved by the 95th Division and proceed directly to Luxembourg and assist the 4th Infantry Division within twenty four hours. Ordering a Division to disengage, turn ninety degrees and move 70 to 80 miles in bad weather and attack in twenty four hours was considered by Military Tacticians to be impossible. Gen. Patton thought it was possible. He said the soldiers could and would do it and he was right. Eighty percent of the Division was in place and ready to attack within twenty four hours after getting the order. The 10th Regiment and the 46th Field Artillery Battalion were the first to move. The Division was well trained and had the equipment to accomplish the move, but the credit should go to the officers and men of the Division. The men were loaded on trucks, tanks, self-propelled guns and Jeeps. They moved at night with headlights on. Lt. Storey and Pfc. Davis both remember the lights being on and commented, "That was the only time they knew that to happen in the war." Vehicles at night used blackout conditions when only a small light in front and back were on. The light was hooded and could not been seen from the air. The weather became cold with light rain as they moved north and the roads was slick making the going difficult. Forty eight hours later the 10th was attacking with the 4th Division in snow and cold. The men were cold, tired and hungry. Pfc. Davis said, 'We were young and by this time of the war, used to such things." Gen. Patton believed the best thing the 10th did was attack soon after arriving in Luxembourg. Gen. Patton when questioned by reporters about the 3rd Army's quick reaction told them, "I had little to do with it. I gave the order and the men did the move and the fighting."

Uncle Wallace wrote on the December 10th saying, "It does not look as if I will be home for Christmas. We have had snow, but have not been real cold yet." A December 19th letter says things have changed and it is very cold with snow and he has not seen the sun for days.

German soldiers who could speak English were recruited and dressed in American uniforms collected from the battlefield. They were given American identification and drove captured American vehicles. The impostors were to infiltrate, get behind American lines and cause confusion. They changed road signs, blew up bridges, broke in on radio transmissions changing orders for the Americans. A rumor was started of plans to capture Gen. Eisenhower, which kept him in his quarters under heavy guard. The Americans soon learned of the imposters and began questioning strangers closely. It was a time to always know the password of the day and who won the last World Series in Baseball.

Bastogne, Belgium was the center of attention as seven roads converge in the small town and the enemy would need to pass through in order to reach their objective. The Ardennes is a hilly, forested area without many roads suitable to carry heavy tanks. The small bridges on the secondary roads would not support the heavy tanks making possibilities limited for the German attack.

The attack came from an area north of Bastogne and along the border of Belgium, south into Luxembourg. The objective of the 5th Division was to keep the attack away from the large city of Luxembourg and to also help the 4th Division. The 4th had been hit hard by the surprise attack and had lost men and equipment.

The 10th Regiment engaged in heavy fighting along the Michelshof-Scheidgan road. On Christmas Eve the 1st Battalion was hit by a counterattack and called in Artillery to control the situation. In bitter cold and snow they push on, never letting the enemy stop. On Christmas Day the 10th was setting

Machine gunner of the 5th Division in Luxembourg during the Battle of the Bulge. Courtesy of the 5th Division in the ETO.

in foxholes looking at the snow covered hills of Luxembourg, reading Gen. Patton's Christmas greeting and the unusual prayer for good weather. Gen Patton had asks the Chaplain of the 3rd Army to write a prayer for good weather. He did, but insisted it would not be well received. The fog lifted and the sun began to shine. Planes started to fly and bring in supplies to those surrounded in Bastogne. Fighter planes were able to find targets of German troops and tanks and aided the Infantry in the fight to stop the attacks.

The 1st Battalion of the 10th had advanced to a ridge overlooking the Sauer River near Echternach. The three Regiments of the 5th with the help of corps artillery had passed through the 4th Division, facing artillery fire, nebelwerfer and rockets. They had stopped the Germans and taken 830 prisoners and recaptured some American equipment.

Major General S. Leroy Irwin, Commander of the 5th received a letter from his wife saying, "I never read anything in the newspapers about the 5th Division." The General wrote back telling her, "We are too busy fighting to worry about publicity." The General assigned Capt. A. B. Campbell to work on news releases for the 5th.

Uncle Wallace wrote on December 30th saying. "We are having real winter weather now. We don't have a lot of wind, like back home. I received a Christmas package from Imogene and Bertha [his sisters]. I have not received yours."

As I was writing part of this story, it began to snow. We had just recuperated from an ice storm. The night temperatures have been down to single digits. On such days I remember the stories about the weather during the Battle of the Bulge. Europe was having the coldest temperatures in fifty years with record amounts of snow. I cannot imagine what it was like to spend all day and night out in such weather. The weather accounted for many casualties, frozen feet and hands were the worst. Many of the wounded froze to death before help could reach them. The men had colds, high fever and pneumonia. The winter clothing issue never arrived as Gen. Bradley did not order any because he thought the war would end before winter.

Sgt. Don Burgett, a member of A Company, 506th Parachute Infantry Regiment of the 101st Airborne Division, remembers the weather and the fighting at Bastogne. He writes. "Every hour of every day of every year I live part of the war. I don't go back as portrayed in the movies or on TV, but thoughts return without my permission and I feel the death and maiming of my comrades. The war and close in battles in the fog and snow laden trees make a battle very close and personal, especially 19, 20, 21 and 22 December 1944." Sgt. Burgett and the 101st Airborne were surrounded in Bastogne for eight days during the time he writes about.

The Germans had been pushed back across the Sauer River by December 30th. The 5th Division held at the river patrolling and keeping the bridges open. The fighting was slow for the first eighteen days of January, giving the Division some rest. The weather remained cold with snow every few days.

During one attack in late December or early January, Lt. Liebner tells about finding an abandoned fifty caliber machine gun, which weighed about one hundred pounds. They had just started an attack, as Lt. Liebner ran by the gun he picked it up, swinging it on his back. They were going downhill and the weight of the gun caused him to go faster than he wanted. He caught his foot on a root growing out of the ground and fell. As he was falling he threw the gun, not wanting it to come down on his back or head. He dislocated his shoulder causing his arm to extend upward. His men thought he was signaling them to stop the attack. The shoulder was put back in place, but he had to have a shoulder replacement in his later years.

After recovering from his wounds sustained in Normandy, Lt. Bud Liebner had returned to C Company and was now leader of the Weapons Platoon. He remembered seeing and talking with Gen. Patton on Christmas day. The General told him they would be attacked and to call for Artillery as they had plenty and they would help. In Gen. Patton's book, "WAR AS I KNEW IT," he writes about visiting elements of the 10th Regiment on Christmas day.

Lt. Storey writes of a Christmas day incident. A Medic, Pfc. Robert W. Cassels, told Lt. Storey he had seen two wounded Germans a little way back. He was asking for permission to go treat their wounds. It was not far and he would hurry. The company rule was for no one to go alone and Lt. Storey knew this, but it was Christmas and he thought Pfc. Cassels was thinking about that and gave him permission to go back and treat the wounds of the enemy. A little latter a platoon leader came asking about Pfc. Cassels and Lt. Storey told him he knew were he was and would check on him. He found Pfc. Cassels beside the wounded Germans shot in the head, presumably by a sniper. Pfc. Jack Davis remembers Pfc. Cassels as a fellow Medic and friend and told the same story. I am sure this incident did not say much about Christmas to either man. This was only one of several atrocities they witnessed during the war.

On Christmas morning Pfc. Davis noticed a man not far from him bleeding profusely from a head wound. He went to help him, but the man said he wanted to shoot one of those SOB's. Davis told him, he was in no shape to shoot anyone and put a pressure bandage on the wound and started moving him to a nearby house. As they walked by a machine gunner, the gunner asks Pfc. Davis to kick a German soldier out in front of his gun and make sure he was dead. The gunner could not depress his machine gun enough to shoot him and his pistol was frozen. Davis kicked the man and he jumped up and threw up his hands; four more close by did the same. A Sergeant came and made them prisoners. Davis went on to the house and properly treated the wounded man. He later looked out of a window and saw about fifteen prisoners in a pen by a barn, several had been playing dead. Years later at a Regimental Reunion guys would call to Pfc. Davis saying, "Jack, kick that guy and see if he is dead." Jack would reply, "No, he is just drunk."

It was Christmas day and things kept happening. The Germans sent over a guy with a white flag. They wanted the Americans to give up. They quickly sent him back with a, NO! The Germans then began a tremendous counterattack. It was repelled, but then what looked like tanks were approaching and they had no antitank guns, the situation soon became dangerous. Lt. England called for Corps Artillery, everything they had available. He was told some shells would fall on their positions, but the Lieutenant had had no choice as the tanks were very close. Everyone got down in their foxholes as deep as possible. German artillery screams, American artillery hisses. The shells came in with a hissing sound and the tanks turned away. Lt. England was right to call for the artillery, saving many lives, but he was killed. Pfc. Davis remembers he was a good officer. The artillery mentioned by Gen. Patton had saved the day for some men of the 10th Regiment.

The next day the 10th counterattacked and captured the man who had brought over the white flag. During the attack, Pfc. Davis was looking for a foxhole, a deep foxhole. He found one with a dead German in it. He pulled him out and started to get in the hole when he noticed an empty Schnapps bottle in the bottom. The soldier smelled of alcohol, the German soldiers had been given a bottle of Schnapps, a Nazi pep talk and told to," Go get those guys." It was a foolish thing for them to do.

Gen. Patton and the 3rd Army had been chosen by Gen. Eisenhower to break through and relieve those surrounded in Bastogne. Gen. Patton sent the 4th Armored Division to lead the attack, assisted by the 26th and 80th Infantry Divisions. The 4th Armored was short of tanks and those they did have were not in good shape due to heavy use. They experienced breakdowns, but never waivered from the assigned mission.

The terrain over which the Infantry units had to fight was roller-coaster, deep hollows and ravines with heavy woods. The cold weather and deep snow made going slow. The foggy weather cleared on December 23rd, allowing fighter planes to help. Bastogne was getting short on supplies and the good flying weather allowed them to receive food, ammunition and medical supplies. Additional Medical teams were flown in by glider.

Gen. Patton tried to give those in Bastogne a Christmas present, but was a little late. The breakthrough happened at 1700 hours on the 26th, Bastogne was relieved.

Uncle Wallace wrote on January 3rd, "I am setting in my foxhole with snow and ice all around; we might go sledding, if we could find a sled. There are some real steep hills to coast down. I am still looking for your Christmas present."

When the fighting slowed in early January, Uncle Wallace had time to write and wrote seven letters before the Sauer River crossing on January 18th. I am sure this time was difficult because of the weather and spending Christmas fighting a war. His mail probably was not arriving with any regularity causing him to feel lonely. The soldiers of World War II endured much, not only the fighting, but the weather conditions in Europe were certainly not like being on a tropical island. They were always looking for a place to warm up, for more sleep and hot food and a hot bath would have been well received. Not having winter clothing was another thing to endure, but most implemented ways of dealing with each situation. Youth was on their side and they were by this time in the war conditioned to hard going.

In early January, near Frombourg, Luxembourg, Pfc. Davis saw six members of the 12th Regiments of the 4th Division that had been captured and shot in the head with their boots re-

Evidence of German atrocities. Six Americans of the 4th Infantry Division were lined up and shot after being captured. Man in the upper right corner of photo is Pfc. Jack Davis. Courtesy of the 5th Division in the ETO.

moved. The men were laid side by side; evidence the enemy was sending a message. This was seen several times in Luxembourg during December and January. The shooting of wounded or captured soldiers was not allowed by the Geneva Convention, which were the rules of war agreed on by countries following World War I. The German Government had signed the agreement, but did not adhere to the rules.

The Americans also signed the agreement, and soldiers were expected to follow the rules. The killing of prisoners was forbidden and was punishable by Court-Martial. The penalty could be imprisonment or they could be shot by a firing squad. Some of the enemy was shot by Americans and happened after witnessing such action by the enemy. Anger came quickly and some men reacted violently and quickly without thinking.

January 5th, "Your last letter said it had been cold back home, it has been pretty much like winter here. We had snow all day yesterday. I hope you raise lots of chickens next year. I sent you a money order by Air-Mail."

January 17th, "I am still in Luxembourg and have not received your Christmas present. I heard some packages were lost. It is probably in that bunch. Same story, it's still snowing."

The 5th Division crossed the Sauer River on January 18th. The 2nd and 3rd Battalions were first to cross in assault boats. The 1st Battalion crossed at 1000 hours near Gilsdorf, Bettendorf and Diekirch with C Company near Diekirch. The entire Division was across by dark, despite the snow and mud. The Engineers were able to span the river with one treadway, two Class 40 and two assault bridges, plus two foot bridges. The 10th was to continue north to the Our River and on to Merescheid and Putscheid. Among the items captured at Metz was some snow ski's which were now attached to litters and made evacuating the wounded fast and easy. The Regiment found five Battalions of enemy Artillery at hill 383 and learned they did not have the means to move the guns. The snow kept falling.

Uncle Wallace wrote his last letter on January 21, 1945. I have not edited or changed any words. The entire letter is as he wrote it.

Dear Mother, Dad and all.

Well I will try to write you all a few lines to let you know that I am well and getting along fine. I hope this finds you all the same. I haven't heard from anyone for quite awhile, except one from Bertha I got day before yesterday and it was wrote December 2nd. Well Mother there is nothing much to write about. Still having plenty of cold weather and it snows about every day. Well mother I just thought I would drop you a few lines to let know I am OK. I am in a hurry so will close for this time hoping to hear from you real soon.

> With Love
> Your son
> Wallace

I am sure the weather had delayed the mail. The confusion of the battle may have been a factor. The tone of the letter seems to indicate he was a bit low at not receiving any letters from his mother and not many from anyone. His family was a source of strength and when letters did not arrive in a timely fashion, along with the weather conditions, being almost in constant combat situations and not knowing if the end was possible, may have made him feel forgotten by those he loved the most.

The 1st Battalion attacked Puhl and about noon C Company was fanning out under a smoke screen. An hour later they had pushed to the top of a hill and into some woods. The fighting continued into the late afternoon and they took some artillery fire. Lt. Storey and two forward observers were under a tree when a shell hit the tree killing the Artillerymen and severely wounding Lt. Storey. Lt. Liebner was in a foxhole not far away and also was badly wounded from the tree burst. Lt. Storey bent down to see how badly the others were hurt, not realizing he had been hit. He could not hear, but did not feel pain at the time. He soon noticed blood dripping on the white camouflage suit he was wearing, from a neck wound. He was given the prescribed treatment of sulfa tablets and sulfa powder was put on the wound and then he was evacuated to an aid station in Diekirch.

Lt. Liebner had been yelling at Lt. Storey and the others,

thinking they were drawing the artillery fire. Lt. Liebner said, "I could feel the debris going in my body." He thinks it was a long time before he was evacuated. Men close by him did not think it was possible for him to live and that may have been the reason evacuation was slow as they practiced triage, meaning those with a possibility to live be sent out first. Lt. Liebner told me the terribly cold weather may have saved his life because blood loss was slow due to the cold. He was evacuated to the aid station in Diekirch.

Lt. Virgil Hawthorne was also hit as he stood up trying to locate the source of the firing and later died from his wounds. Pfc. Davis had talked to him just days before and the Lieutenant had told him it was his thirty fifth birthday, but he did not think he would make it to thirty six. This did not sound like him as he was always optimistic. Lt. Hawthorne had been in the army for several years and was older than most. Pfc. Davis said, "He was my favorite platoon leader."

The Jeep taking Lt. Storey to the aid station got stuck in the snow, but with the help of nearby troopers was finally dug out and sent on to the aid station. From Diekirch Lt. Storey was taken to Luxembourg City for surgery and stayed several days. He remembers in the receiving area of the hospital smelling perfume as a pretty brunette nurse came with a pair of scissors to cut off his uniform. He told the nurse the smell of the perfume was the best thing to happen so far. A few days earlier he had gotten a new GI sweater, replacing the dirty, smelly one he had worn for a long time. The first article of clothing the nurse cut away was the new sweater. She explained they had to quickly get ready for surgery. Lt. Storey also had leg wounds in addition to the neck wound. He was then sent to Paris in a boxcar with a wood stove for heat. The hospital ran out of pajamas and Lt. Storey went to Paris naked covered only with scratchy blankets captured from the German Army and developed scabies. The Doctors said the scabies were caused by the blankets. The last hospital was in England for more surgery and recovery. The war in Europe was over when he was released from the hospital. Lt. Storey had a photo taken in England and sent it to his parents to let them know he was not disfigured by the wounds.

Lt. Liebner was in the hospital at Diekirch for ten days and could hear sounds of the battle occurring not far away. He was then sent to a General Hospital and thought he received excellent care. The war ended as Lt. Liebner was returning to C Company. He would later develop problems from the wounds and spend months in an Army Hospital in Clinton, Iowa.

The 1st Battalion pushed on toward the small village of Putscheid. Putscheid was in a hilly, partly wooded area on the west side of the Our River and was being held by the enemy with self propelled guns and tanks operating in and around the town. Artillery fire from Weiler helped them continue stiff resistance. Supporting armor shelled Putscheid as A Company prepared to enter the town. A Company moved to the draw that led into the town and was stopped by machine gun fire. The German army was using a road that ran through Putscheid taking them back to Germany after the failed attempt in the Ardennes. Battered elements of another division had made attempts to take Putscheid, but were stopped each time they tried. The Germans fought hard to keep Putscheid as they needed the road to get men and equipment back to Germany. The German border is less than two miles from Putscheid.

Pfc. Davis remembers it was very cold during this time, only six or eight degrees above zero. He was wearing three pairs of woolen underwear, olive drab pants, shirt and sweater and a driver's coat. He had two pairs of socks; one he kept dry under his clothes, while wearing the other pair. The gloves he had were thin and did not keep out the cold. He suffers from frozen feet and hands to this day.

After A Company's withdrawal, the 1st Battalion remained in position preparing to renew the attack on Putscheid. On January 27th a patrol was sent out and got within twenty five yards of the town. They were discovered and chased away with machine gun fire. While preparing for the attack, Cpl. Tom Tucker and three other members of B Company's 7th Combat Engineer Battalion plowed open the road from Diekirch to Putscheid in the dark and received enemy fire from 88mm guns. The snow was knee deep and staying on the road was difficult. Supplies were moved over the road as well as tanks and it was used to evacuate wounded to the field hospital in Diekirch.

It was C Company's job to attack Putscheid and the attack started at 0600 hours on the 28th with fog and light snow. They had to cross over the high side of a draw leading into the town exposing them to the enemy. They moved over the hump and were soon pinned down in front of the town by small arms, mortar and tanks or self propelled guns. The enemy counterattacked and drove the leading elements of C Company to the bottom of the draw where well placed machine guns pinned them and they could not move forward or withdraw. Artillery was called, but it was impossible due to fog and light snow to adjust fire on the machine guns. About one platoon including Lt. Robert Neale, Company Commander, three platoon leaders and the forward observer for artillery were captured. C Company lost sixteen men killed in the attack, the worst loss for the company in a single day during the war. Lt. Robert Dunn, the only remaining officer organized what was left of the company, setting up machine guns to keep the attack going. The remaining troops were finally able to withdraw. At the end of the day Putscheid was in control of the 1st Battalion.

Among the sixteen men who lost their lives that day were Pfc. Melvin Wallace Dunn and two of his friends, Sgt. Phillip Clover and Pfc. John Chichilla. The war ended for them on a cold, snowy day, Sunday, January 28, 1945.

SSgt. August Reinhart was captured and as they marched him away, he noticed Pfc. Marvin Cummings lying on the ground apparently dead. For some reason Sgt. Reinhart knew Cummings was only playing dead and as he was walking by, put his finger up to his lips, signaling Cummings to be still. When things got quiet Cummings crawled back to a place where he could stand up then ran out of the battle area.

The German army suffered terribly as they retreated. Fighter bombers attacked the road back to the German border and the destroyed vehicles lined the road like a fence. The official dates for the Battle of the Bulge are December 16th to January 25th. After studying the war, most historians think the battle ended on January 28th when the 10th Regiment took Putscheid. Many times during the war, the army released to the press word that a battle was over, before all was secure. The news would be on the front page of newspapers back home causing all to feel good.

During the fighting around Putscheid, Pfc. Davis was in a foxhole with fellow trooper Art Williams. Williams was never afraid of anything. They were getting fire from enemy tanks. An American tank destroyer pulled up next to their foxhole and tank destroyers always drew fire. Williams said to Pfc. Davis, "It is suicide to stay here, let's get out and go behind that hill." Pfc. Davis had always been told that when a person is really scared, their feet get cold and his feet were very cold. They got out of the hole and started back, but Davis could hardly move and Williams got hold of him and got him started. Davis said, "What scared me the most was Williams being scared. I thought if he is scared, what should I be?" Pfc. Davis said, I was in some close situations, but I have never been that scared."

Putscheid is a small village and is north of Luxembourg City, about fifty minutes driving time. It seems too small to have been the location of a significant battle of World War II. The people of Luxembourg still remember what the 5th Division did for them in the war and today hold ceremonies each year honoring them. Family members of the men in the division who return are given red carpet treatment. They have not forgotten the war and the men who fought it.

While touring Europe in 1998, our tour bus took us within three miles of the American Cemetery at Hamm near Luxembourg City. I could not find a way to visit the cemetery. The tour had stopped at the cemetery for many years, but due to complaints had discontinued stopping, because tour members did not want to look at graves. They did not want to spend a few minutes honoring those who gave their lives for the freedom they have enjoyed for sixty plus years.

Pfc. Melvin Wallace Dunn is buried at Hamm, Luxembourg along with 5,075 others. Most are from the Battle of the Bulge and a unit of the 3rd Army. All fifty states and the District of Columbia are represented. Twenty two brothers rest side by side and there are 101 unknowns. General George S. Patton Jr. is buried there; he was not killed in the war, but died as the result of an automobile accident after the war in Germany in December 1945.

The cemetery consist of fifty acres of land given to the United

States to bury their war dead. It is a peaceful, beautiful place with well cared for grounds. On a memorial set in granite paving, with bronze letters are the words:

> ALL WHO SHALL HEREAFTER LIVE IN FREEDOM WILL BE HERE REMINDED
> THAT TO THESE MEN AND THEIR COMRADES WE OWE A DEBT TO BE PAID
> WITH GRATEFUL REMEMBERANCE OF THEIR SACRAFICE AND WITH HIGH
> RESOLVE THAT THE CAUSE FOR WHICH THEY DIED SHALL LIVE ETERNALLY

My tears are on this page, for which I offer no apology. My gratitude is eternal for the men and women who fought in World War II. It was the job of some to man the fighter planes and bombers in the skies, others fought on the beaches in

Melvin Dunn's headstone in the American Cemetery in Hamm, Luxembourg. Courtesy of John Parton.

Normandy, in the rain and mud of Northern France and in the snow and cold of Belgium and Luxembourg. Women served, mostly as nurses and were often near the front. They were wounded or killed when the hospitals were shelled. Others performed jobs in support of those in combat, in the air, on the water and on the ground. All were important to accomplishing victory.

The Battle of the Bulge involved 600,000 Americans. The casualties totaled 81,000 of which 15,000 were captured and 19,000 were killed. The British employed 55,000 troops with total casualties of 1,400 of which 200 were killed. About ten million Americans were involved in the war in Europe, of that number only one and a half million actually saw combat. The others were in support of the effort.

In 1994, Pfc. Davis returned to Europe for the 50th Anniversary of the war. He went to the cemetery in Luxembourg and found the graves of several of his comrades. One grave he visited was of Lt. Virgil Hawthorne, his favorite platoon leader. Lt. Hawthorne had told Pfc. Davis on his thirty fifth birthday, he would not make it to the thirty sixth and he was right.

9

GERMANY AND HOME

In early February the Allies started what most veterans call the push. Gen. Eisenhower had maintained the strategy of a broad front assault beginning with the landings in Normandy. He chose to continue this after the Battle of the Bulge. The German Army had not penetrated the allied line with their attack through the Ardennes and was now retreating back to Germany and behind the Siegfried Line. Gen. Eisenhower wanted to keep up the pressure and all Divisions were ordered to attack.

Gen. Montgomery thought the Germans were preparing for another massive attack and counseled Gen. Eisenhower to wait and see what happened. Gen. Eisenhower did not accept this and the push began. Gen. Montgomery was a meticulous planner and did not want to start an attack before all things were in place. Any delay would give the enemy time to set up a defensive line behind the Siegfried line, or West Wall, and Gen. Eisenhower knew this would happen.

Exhausted divisions, short of men and equipment followed orders and the push started early in February. The drive was on to push the German army back and across the Rhine River.

During the drive to Putscheid, the 10th had advanced from positions on the north bank of the Sauer River, to a line southwest of the Our River, forming a line extending from the high ground west of Putscheid to the high ground northwest of Vianden. In Northern Luxembourg are the Our, Sure and the Sauer Rivers. The Our River flows from the north and joins the Sure flowing from the west and together they form the Sauer running along the border of Luxembourg and Germany. I was talking with Lt. Liebner about the rivers in Luxembourg and told him how they came together. He suddenly said, "I was there and never understood how they flowed until now. We crossed a lot of rivers during the war." The 5th Division crossed twenty three rivers causing Gen. Patton to say, "You all must have web feet." The river they all wanted to cross was the Rhine as it would mean they were into Germany and possibly close to the end of the war. About six weeks later the 10th did cross the Rhine River on March 23, 1945.

The Battle of the Bulge had left the German army scattered and confused. They had lost thousands of men, killed, wounded or captured. Company size was down to seventy men of the usual 150. They had fighter planes, but no fuel or Pilots.

In early February the 10th was positioned north of Hoscheid facing the Sauer River. About 150 yards back from the far shore were enemy pillboxes and back of them were more pillboxes with tanks and infantry. A crossing was made by E Company and several boats were sunk, but the 10th would not give up. The men, who were not killed or wounded, swam back and got in another boat and continued until they were across.

During the night of 11-12 February the 1st Battalion's C Company reached Bollendorf and cleared the town. The pillboxes were by-passed and attacked from the rear. The pillboxes were designed for guns to be placed and fired only from the front. The infantry attacked from the rear, placing TNT charges at the back door destroying them.

The 5th Division was ordered to be part of the 3rd Army's drive to clear the area to Trier and Bitburg. They again had to cross the Sauer River. I have not counted the number of times they crossed the Sauer, but they must hold a record for crossing the same river during the war. The Engineers erected a foot bridge across the Prum River and the Division crossed that river. As the 5th Division Artillery was shelling Peffingen and the hill beyond, two additional bridges were thrown across the river along with a vehicular bridge late in the afternoon. The Nims River was next, but before crossing the town of Messerich had to be cleared. The Nims River goes through Messerich and the bridge had been destroyed by the enemy, but it was discovered the troops could cross on the rubble. The Engineers erected a class 40 bridge and operations were greatly accelerated.

The 1st Battalion cleared Esslingen and both sides of the Trier-Bitburg road. They continued the advance, clearing Rohl and all resistance to the Kyll River. After a short fire fight the 1st was in Gondorf where they were relieved on March 10th.

The 10th was close to the Moselle River by March 13th and from this point they would chase the enemy all the way to the Rhine River near Worms. They then moved south driving the enemy out of the Saar Basin. It was now apparent the German Army was trying to get all troops over the Rhine, before all bridges were blown. March 17th the 1st Battalion was loaded on trucks and crossed the Moselle River and cleared a route south of Gemunden and moved on to Bingert and a spot near Bad Kreuznach by the West Wall. In the past nine days the 3rd Army had taken 100,000 prisoners.

Supplies and man power for the crossing of the Rhine had been given to British Gen. Montgomery and the attached American 9th Army for a crossing at Wesel in the north. Gen Patton wanted his 3rd Army to be first to cross the Rhine River and as they got closer, he made plans for sneaking across at a site near Oppenheim. They would try without the usual bombing and shelling of the far shore. The push was on the 3rd Army to reach the river before the enemy knew they were in the area. Pfc. Davis remembers how hard they were pushed. He said, "We were very tired, but the orders were to keep going." Gen. Patton had chosen the 5th Division to be first of the 3rd Army to cross. The 5th past performance in crossing rivers was well known in the 3rd Army.

The first crossing of the Rhine River by the Allies was accomplished by the 9th Armored Division at Remagen on March 7th. Remagen is south of Oppenheim and was not considered to be a good place to cross because the far bank was steep and not suitable for wheeled vehicles. The 9th had been in good tank country and had made fast progress. Brigadier General William Hoge had kept his command moving fast, knowing the enemy could not set up a defensive line. He believed it was the best way to win the war.

From a hill behind Remagen, the leading elements of the 9th Armored discovered the Ludendorff Railroad Bridge still standing. Intelligence thought all bridges over the Rhine River had been bombed by the Allies or blown by the Germans. The 9th came to Remagen on a tar covered road and paused by the Apollinaris Church to make plans for crossing. They knew it was important to take the bridge quickly, before their presence was discovered. The job of taking the bridge was given to Lt. Karl Timmermann, commander of the 9th Divisions A Company. Lt. Timmermann was concerned they would be discovered and the Germans would blow the bridge as the company approached. This had happened to one company of the 101st Airborne in Holland while fighting with Gen. Montgomery's British forces. The 101st had orders to take a bridge over the Wilhelmina Canal near Son and as they approached the bridge was blown in their face.

The Ludendorff Bridge at Remagen was constructed in 1916 during World War I for rail and foot traffic. The railroad came through Remagen, across the bridge and through a tunnel on the east side of the river. The ground rises sharply on the east side of the river making the tunnel necessary. The hill or small mountain is called the Erpeler Ley.

Lt. Timmermann was from Nebraska, but was born in Ger-

The remains of the Ludendorff Bridge at Remagen on the east side of the Rhine River. Courtesy of the author.

many. His father was a soldier with the American Army in World War I. His mother grew up in Frankfurt, Germany, where the couple met after the war and were married. When Lt. Timmermann was eighteen months old the family came to the States and settled in Nebraska. I have wondered if Lt. Timmermann and his parents had once crossed the bridge by train when he was a baby. As Lt. Timmermann and A Company approached the bridge, the Germans tried to blow it up, but the attempt failed. The approach on the west side had a big hole and part way across, along one side was another hole. Lt. Timmermann and Sgt. Drabek led the company across amid machine gun and rifle fire. They were the first Americans to cross the Rhine River during the war. Both were awarded the Distinguished Service Cross for their action that day. The German Army did not have a force of any size at Remagen and the 9th Armored soon had control of the bridge.

The Engineers repaired the bridge and the Americans began crossing. They quickly had enough men and equipment across to establish a bridgehead. The enemy tried firing artillery at the bridge to collapse it and also sent divers down the river to set charges underwater. The divers were discovered before getting near the bridge. The enemy also sent bombers to destroy the bridge, but this was not successful. The combination of shelling, along with the heavy traffic finally caused the bridge to collapse ten days later. The Engineers had placed pontoon bridges across the river and the crossing of men and equipment did not stop. The complete story of the Rhine crossing at Remagen can be found in Ken Hechler's book, "The Bridge at Remagen."

In 1998, I visited Remagen; all that is left of the bridge are the twin towers on each side of the river. The tunnel has been closed for several years. A company tried raising mushrooms there after the war. Little evidence remains of the bridge or the accomplishment of Lt. Timmermann and Sgt. Drabek and the brave men they led on March 7, 1945.

In the north Gen. Montgomery was preparing to cross the Rhine at Wesel. He had assembled 250,000 men, thirty division from three armies, 37,000 British and 22,000 American Engineers. The Navy provided ocean going assault boats. The

Air Corps would fly 7,000 sorties, dropping 50,000 tons of bombs and the Artillery had 2,000 guns capable of firing 1,000 rounds per minute. He had also arranged for paratroopers to be dropped the day after the crossing. When all was ready the shelling and bombing began, completely destroying Wesel. After the shelling the river was crossed and a bridgehead quickly established.

Gen. Patton had moved the 5th Division up to the river and was ready to start crossing. The 11th Regiment was chosen to be first and began crossing at 2200 hours on March 22nd near Niestein. The river was 800 yards wide at this point and the

Men of the 5th Division in Frankfurt, Germany in late March 1945. Courtesy of the Society of the Fifth Division.

first company paddled across without a shot being fired. The crossing continued for two hours before enemy artillery fired a few rounds, but no concentrated firing was done by the enemy.

The 10th Regiment began crossing at 0200 hours on the 23rd. The 1st Battalion was first followed by the others and all were across by 0700. The 1st Battalion headed toward Leesheim and C Company met some resistance from small arms, but soon captured most of the enemy that had fired on them. The 3rd Battalion was near Nauheim with the rest spread out to expand the bridgehead toward Frankfurt and Darmstadt.

On March 26th, the 10th crossed the Main River into Frankfurt. C Company took the Rhine-Main Airport and found eight German planes intact. They then continued the attack into Schwanheim, a suburb of Frankfurt.

Frankfurt was the ninth largest city in Germany with a population of about 500,000 and had been repeatedly bombed by the Allies. The bombing severely damaged the city and may account for the reactions of the citizens, who caused more problems for the troops than the German Army. By April 1st, Frankfurt had been cleared and the 10th was enjoying a beautiful spring day with plenty of sunshine.

The 10th was inactive for the next four days and troops walked the streets enjoying the weather, no snow, no rain, but warm sunshine. The trees were about to leaf out and flowers were blooming, reminding the soldiers of their Grandmother or Mothers garden back home.

Pfc. Davis remembers Bill Cross a man from Harlan County, Kentucky was shot in the stomach at Frankfurt. Davis said, "He must have had nine lives as he had been shot twice before the war, once by his father during a fight." Davis also remembers another man from Pennsylvania who thought war was fun. He had been hit in September and had returned to the 10th only to be riddled by machine gun fire.

Orders were received to move north toward Giessen and then on to the Ruhr River. It was another hurry up move and the 10th again went first, such as they did when moving to Luxembourg for the Battle of the Bulge in December. The soldiers rode on anything with wheels, but the vehicles had seen heavy use and were beginning to break down, needing maintenance before covering the required 100 miles.

Short of manpower and some equipment the 10th cleared the town of Meschede. C Company captured Hellefeld receiving seven casualties. They were at Husten by April 13th, where five bridges crossed the tributary of the Ruhr River. Lt. Robert Dunn, commander of C Company and his radio operator went on one of the bridges and cut wires to explosives, before the enemy could blow the bridge.

From April 15th to the 22nd, the 1st Battalion patrolled gathering stragglers in the Ruhr Pocket. The German soldiers were given instructions by their officers to escape the best way possible. Some were given discharge papers and changed to civilian clothes, but most were caught and made a prisoner. Others knew the war was lost and surrendered when approached and made no effort to escape.

Adjustments were being made in Command structure during April. Officers were promoted and moved to new responsibilities. Col. Robert Bell, who had commanded the 10th Regiment since before Normandy was moved to Division. Lt. Col. Frank Langfitt Jr. had been commander of the 1st Battalion was made executive officer of the 10th Regiment and Major Wilfrid Haughey was promoted to commander of the 1st Battalion.

In late April the 5th Division began a move toward Czechoslovakia. The Division was kept busy clearing their assigned zones without much difficulty. The German soldiers wanted to surrender to the American or British army before the Russians could capture them. They all knew they would receive better treatment. The weather turned disagreeable as they neared Czechoslovakia with cold rain and snow in the mountains.

Gen. Eisenhower had made the decision in March to let the Russian Army capture Berlin. The Allies were 200 miles from Berlin and the Russians only thirty five miles from the capitol city. The decision caused much controversy among the Allies, but Gen. Eisenhower claimed Berlin was no longer a Military Target and was at best a political prize. The Russians wanted the honor of capturing Berlin and Gen. Eisenhower was happy to let them. It was estimated that capturing Berlin would cost 100,000 more casualties, a high price to pay. Another reason for the Allies not to take Berlin was the decision made at a conference in Malta by President Roosevelt, British Prime Minister Churchill and Russian Prime Minister Stalin during February. They had set the zones of occupation and most of Berlin was in the Russian zone.

The Allies were to stop at the Elbe River and wait to link up with the Russian Army. Gen. Simpson's 9th Army arrived at the Elbe by the middle of April. The flow of German soldiers and civilians kept the 9th Army busy. None of the Germans wanted to be under the control of the Russians.

Adolph Hitler committed suicide in his underground bunker in Berlin on April 30th and the German Army's high command soon made plans for surrender.

On May 2nd the 10th Regiment had troops in Germany, Austria and Czechoslovakia. When the war ended the 1st Battalion was in Winterberg, Czechoslovakia. The Germans signed papers for the unconditional surrender on May 7, 1945. The time was 0241 hours and the signing took place in a school house in Reims, France. The war was over and the shooting stopped. Those still alive and not wounded were extremely happy it was over, but the end did not turn into a hilarious, rowdy occasion. Most were tired of the war with memories of buddies killed or wounded. No one felt like throwing a party.

The 10th Regiment had a few days to rest, but soon went back to training. The war with Japan was not over and the 5th Division had been ordered to the Pacific after returning to the States. They were to get thirty days leave and report for shipment to another war. Inspections stiffened and the foxhole look soon disappeared.

During the last week of the war Pfc. Jack Davis had not been feeling well. He found out he had hepatitis and was sent to a hospital in Reims, France. He was reading the Stars and Stripes, the Army newspaper and read an article saying the 5th Division was going home. He wanted to go with them and talked his way out of the hospital arriving back at the Division as they were preparing to load out.

The 83rd Infantry Division relieved the 5th Division on June

12, 1945 and the 5th began the long move back to LeHarve, France loaded on box cars. They made a short stop in Reims at Camp St. Louis. Pfc. Davis could see the hospital where he had been a few days earlier. The 5th arrived at Camp Lucky Strike and made preparations for boarding the S.S. Sea Porpoise, leaving France on July 10, 1945. The crossing took eight days on a calm sea and the men listened to popular music of the time that most had only heard about. It was a relaxing trip and the men had time to talk, sleep and eat. The S.S. Sea Porpoise docked in New York, during a heavy rainstorm on July 18, 1945. The 5th was home after a long war and the men were excited about getting to see their families again.

They spent two or three days at Camp Shanks before being sent to Recuperation Centers near their homes. After having health checks and completing some paper work, they were allowed to spend thirty days home before returning to Camp Campbell, Kentucky. The 5th Division had been selected for duty in the Pacific Theater to fight the Japanese. The Atomic Bomb saved them from doing this as the war in the Pacific was over when they returned to Camp Campbell.

After a thirty day furlough the men of the 10th Regiment returned to Camp Campbell and waited for discharge. The time went slow until all the paperwork was done and they were on their way back home to an uncertain life. Returning to civilian life was difficult for most as the war had changed them in ways unimaginable. They were asked questions about the war and when they responded most did not believe what they had to say about the war and what they experienced. This caused most to not talk about the war, unless in the company of another veteran. Their response to others was, "I just did my job." Or perhaps, "I am not a hero, because all the hero's are in the cemeteries." Most did not tell their families about their war experiences for about fifty years and only began to talk after the 50th Anniversary passed and several books were written about the war and the men who fought it. Their children were surprised to learn Grandpa or Dad was in the war. Most found no glory in war, only death and destruction. They were proud to have served, but never wanted to do it again.

Lt. Harold Storey did not return with the Division as he had been in England in the hospital recovering from wounds. Lt. Storey was given orders, with the help of two other officers, the job of establishing a trade school for Europeans in England. The school was eight weeks in length and accommodated 4000 students, who were taught to operate heavy equipment. He remained in this duty for a few months until receiving orders to return to the States.

In early winter Lt. Storey boarded the Lake Champlain, an aircraft carrier, which was new and had not been in the war. While crossing the Atlantic, they were caught in bad winter storm and had to devise a snowplow to clear the decks. They may have barely moved in one twenty four hour period. He arrived in New York to Camp Kilmer and was released on furlough. The weather was cold and the facilities on the train taking him to Georgia were frozen and the train had to stop several times for the passengers to use restrooms and get food and water. He arrived in the early morning of Christmas Eve at Ft. Gordon, Georgia. His parents were there to meet him and after the necessary paper work, they were on the way home.

It became dark as they drove toward home and a light rain was falling, which caused ice to form on the road. A car hit them causing his mother a cut on her knee and his father received bruised ribs. The car was damaged and had to be towed. A Greyhound bus stopped and his parents rode the bus into town. Lt. Storey stayed and got a wrecker to take the car off the highway. He remembers having to pay a Christmas Eve price for the wrecker service.

After his furlough, Lt. Storey went to Ft. Gordon to await discharge. He learned of his promotion to Captain, which had come through while he was in the hospital recovering from wounds. The papers had finally caught up with him. He was discharged in February 1946 and joined a reserve unit. He was called back for the Korean War, but was rejected three times because of the wounds received in World War II.

The men were again civilians and would be busy with families and careers, but memories of the war have remained with them though the years. More than sixty years have passed, but

L-R, Bill Ellis, 7th Combat Engineers, Tom Tucker, 7th Combat Engineers and Jack Davis, Medic in the 10th Infantry Regiment at a hunting lodge in the Pocono Mountains in Pennsylvania fifty years after the war. All veterans of the fighting at Metz, France. Courtesy of Jack Davis.

Lt's Byron and Lucille Liebner shortly after they were married in 1946. Courtesy of Lucille Liebner.

some have vivid memories of what they endured. Names of the men they fought with may be gone, but not their young faces. I have mentioned some names to them and they always reply, "I have not thought about him for years." Stories will follow and more names are remembered, those memories tell the history of the biggest war ever fought.

Men of the 10th Regiment at a reunion several years after the war. 3rd man from the left is Warren Mullins and man in wheel chair is Gus Reinhart. Courtesy of Lucille Liebner.

10

FRIENDS

Most who served in World War II had friends that also served. Uncle Wallace was no exception in this regard and I was able to learn of a few and interview their families. They had known each other from school or as neighbors; others became friends after entering the military. During my research I made contact with Sandra MacDuffee, whose father, Pfc. John Chichilla was in my Uncles Platoon and was killed in the same battle. Sandra had posted a message on AWON, American World War II Orphans Network, a web site dedicated to those whose fathers were killed in the war. She wanted to find anyone with information about the 5th Division's battle at Putscheid, Luxembourg. I contacted AWON and they put us in touch. Sandra sent me a small history of C Company, along with some photos. Sandra and her husband visited Luxembourg in 2001 and again in 2009. She told me all she knew about her father.

John Chichilla grew up in Pennsylvania, the only boy of five children. He was thirty three years old when drafted for service with the army. He reported to C Company as a replacement in September 1944 and was in the 1st Platoon.

Sandra's mother kept all the letters from her husband and after the war gave them to his sister, when she remarried. About fifty years later the Aunt sent the letters to Sandra and she then started a search to learn more about her father's time in the Army. She has searched for years trying to find anyone who knew her father during the war.

Memorial Day ceremonies in Luxembourg at the American Military Cemetery are held each year in June. The veterans or their family members are given red carpet treatment by the local people. They are happy to take family members to the

Cemetery or to the battle site at Putscheid and tell them about what took place there in January 1945. Sandra stood on the ground where C Company was pinned down and walked in Scheid Woods where the Company spent the night before the battle. This was an emotional time for Sandra and a trip she will never forget.

While at the Cemetery Sandra took photos of her father's headstone as well as one of Wallace Dunn's. She sent me copies of the photos of the Cemetery and the area where the battle occurred.

I have asked all the men of C Company if they remember Pfc. John Chichilla and none think they do. Sandra was two years old when her Father was killed and does not remember him. Her struggle to find anyone who knew him during the war will continue.

Among the letters from Uncle Wallace were five dated from January through March 1945 from Mrs. Bud Clover. In the mid 1990's at a Dunn Family dinner, my sister along with oth-

Pfc. John Chichilla with daughter Sandra. Courtesy of Sandra MacDuffee.

ers was reading the letters from Uncle Wallace and discovered the letters from Mrs. Clover. My sister worked with a lady named Clover and remembered her telling about her husband's Grandmother and that she admired her for raising two boys after their father was killed in World War II. When my sister returned to work, she told the lady about the letters and my search began to learn about Phillip Clover.

Phillip Clover, or Bud, was a replacement in C Company in September 1944. My Uncle had written in a letter dated September 30, 1944 about a man from Northern Oklahoma joining his squad a few days past. We now know that man was Bud Clover. Bud was thirty four years old when he was drafted in early 1944. He was the father of two sons, Stanley and Bradford, ages eleven and thirteen.

I met with Brad on a cold winter day and while having coffee and hot chocolate he told me about his father. They all thought he would not be drafted because of his age and having two children. He was sent to Camp Fannin at Tyler, Texas for Basic Training. Mrs. Clover and the boys moved to Tyler to be with him while he was in training. Stanley and Brad became good friends with some neighbor boys. They planned to go fishing one day, but their friend's father had other plans. He wanted them to plant some beans in the garden and then go fishing. The four boys planted two rows of beans and decided that was enough. They put the extra beans in a hole and covered them. They were soon exposed as the beans sprouted in a few days showing what they had done.

Brad and his brother had the mumps during this time and wanted their father to get them also and maybe he would not have to be shipped overseas. It was not to be and Bud Clover left for Europe on August 2, 1944.

Bud Clover was older than most of the men in the Company and he was called, Pops, and the younger men looked up to him. He was soon promoted to Sergeant, probably because of his age and maturity. His letters to his wife must have talked about some of the men in the Company and how he became friends with them. My Uncle must have been one he wrote about and this is the reason Mrs. Clover wrote to my Grandmother in early January 1945. Fifty years had past and another friendship began with the Clover family.

Sgt. Bud Clover was killed at Putscheid and his family received notice of him missing in action, which was the method used by the army, even if they already knew the soldier had been killed. Mrs. Clover wrote my Grandmother asking about my Uncle and learned he too was missing. The sad day soon came and both families knew the truth, that both men had been killed at Putscheid.

Brad has tried to find someone who had served with his father. He learned of a reunion of those who had trained at Camp Fannin and wrote a letter to be passed around at the reunion. None knew his father, but one man sent him a book he had written about the training at Camp Fannin.

Brad Clover is retired from the Fire Department of our city and is proud of his son, Phillip who is Chief of the De-

Homer Clover visiting his brothers grave in the original American Cemetery in Luxembourg. Courtesy of Brad Clover.

partment. Phillip thinks it is special to have his Grandfather's name.

Sandra MacDuffee and Brad Clover got to know each other in a telephone conversation. They were both children when their fathers were killed in the war and have much in common. Sandra urged Brad to go to Luxembourg and during the summer of 2004, Brad, his wife and daughter flew to Luxembourg and spent several days. They went to Putscheid and saw the area where his father fought and died. They talked with people who remember the war and found out how much the men were appreciated for liberating them during the war. They visited the Cemetery and took photos of my Uncle's headstone. Brad brought a copy of the photo one day and told me because of my interest in his father and the trip to Luxembourg, he finally felt closure after many years.

Brad has given me copies of photo's his Uncle Homer Clover took of the original cemetery and of his father's grave during the war. The Clover family had the remains of Sgt. Phillip

Sgt. Phillip E. Clover. Courtesy of Brad Clover.

E. Clover returned to the states after the war. He is buried at Hawley, Oklahoma where the community has erected a memorial to their war dead.

In 1946 the families of all those killed in the war were given the option of returning the remains of their family member home or having them remain in a permanent cemetery near where they were killed. There were 233,181 war dead returned to the states for burial at a site chosen by the family. The Government paid all the expenses and provided an honor guard to accompany the casket to the final place of burial. Other families believed it was fitting to have their family member buried overseas near the place they fought and died, to rest forever with their comrades. The American Battle Monuments Commission oversees the management of the cemeteries for 93,242 war dead not returned to the United States after the war. There are also 8,000 unknowns buried overseas. These are bodies recovered, but never indentified. Listed as missing were more than 78,000 at the end of the war. In the past sixty or more years some have been found and identified. The World War I and II cemeteries are closed to further burials except for those found and identified from those wars. The number of dead and missing is beyond one's comprehension.

In my Uncle's letters the name Junior Hyde is mentioned several times. Junior was a friend from Mulhall, Oklahoma; they had known each other for several years. The path to war was the same for both men as they went to Camp McCain for training and to Europe on the same ship. Once they were in Europe they became separated and Uncle Wallace wrote asking his mother if she knew where Junior was stationed.

Junior must have been a few weeks ahead of my Uncle in training at Camp McCain as Junior was the first to go home on furlough and told Uncle Wallace it did not take long to get to Mulhall by train. They must have been able to visit a few times at Camp McCain, probably during a pass to one of the small towns in the area.

Sisters Blanche Hill and Pat Allen told me about their brother and his growing up years in Mulhall. Junior, born April 28, 1924, seems to have been a typical youth of the time. He delivered newspapers in Mulhall and Blanche remembers having to do the job for him when he broke his ankle. Most of the route was not bad, except the crossing of the railroad tracks to deliver to the Mulhall Ranch on the west side of town. It was summer when she took over and after crossing the tracks, was tired and sweating. Lucille Mulhall, whose father the town was named for, would see her coming and have a glass of iced tea waiting. Sister Pat Allen was envious of her brother because he had a lot of curly black hair. She said, "It was beautiful." We asked our mother, "Why did Junior get the curly hair?"

Mulhall became a town in 1889 when land was free to those who made the run and staked a claim. Juniors' Grandfather was part of those arriving to develop the community. Juniors' father, Clarence and Uncle Walter served in World War I. Many men in World War II were sons of the men in the First World War.

Rachel [Rundel] Stephenson relates an event that happened in Mulhall. The Rundell family operated a Drug Store in Mulhall for many years. Drug Stores of the time always had a soda fountain that served cold drinks and ice cream. The Rundells noticed when they opened for the day, a dirty ice cream dish and spoon on the counter. This was unusual and it happened

Right and Above: Sgt. Clarence J. Hyde. Courtesy of Blanche Hill.

several times. Nothing else was disturbed, only the dirty dish and spoon was left. They notified the night policeman and he began watching the Drug Store during the night wanting to catch the person who liked ice cream. One morning when the Rundells open the store, they saw a carton of ice cream setting on the counter and it had not melted. They then knew someone was stopping in the early morning and not during the night. They discovered Junior during his rounds delivering the papers would occasionally stop for ice cream. He was getting in through a place in the back of the store, which Rachel said was not hard to do, and enjoying a dish of ice cream before finishing his paper route. Rachel does not remember what punishment he received, but it was probably not harsh.

When war was declared in 1941, Junior was in high school and not old enough to volunteer. He wanted to serve and talked his parents into signing papers allowing him to volunteer. Blanche did not think her parents wanted him to go, but finally gave in and signed the papers.

Junior Hyde and Wallace Dunn were both in the 5th Infantry Division, but in different Regiments. They were surprised to learn this one day when they happened to see each other in Northern Ireland. Sometime during training or after arriving in France, Junior was promoted to Sergeant. During the fighting for Metz, Junior was severely wounded when he was hit by shrapnel, removing part of his jaw bone and lodging in the roof of his mouth. He was evacuated to England by plane and then back to the States, spending a long time in the Army Hospital at Fort Leonard Wood, Missouri. Pat remembers the family traveling there to visit him.

After the war Junior was discharged and returned to Mulhall. He went back to high school and graduated. This was common among veterans who were under age and volunteered for service prior to finishing high school. He suffered from pain caused by the wound for the rest of his life. Blanche told me he was able to live a reasonably normal life and became the father of three daughters and one son. He died April 20, 1989, eight days before his sixty fifth birthday.

Early in my research I was told Junior was killed in the war. I found the name Lt. Earnest C. Hyde Jr. in the list of

KIA's of the 5th Division and assumed he was the Junior Hyde from Mulhall, Oklahoma. I did not know his name was Clarence J. Hyde and the family had always called him Junior. I assumed he had been selected for training at the Officer Candidate School and that explained why my Uncle did not know where he was for a time. When they saw each other in Northern Ireland, it seemed to all fit. More research revealed Lt. Ernest C. Hyde Jr. was from Alabama. The 5th Division National Historian found the truth and informed me Sgt. Clarence J. Hyde from Mulhall, Oklahoma was in the 2nd Regiment of the 5th Division and was wounded at Metz, France.

Credit must be given to Rachael Stephenson for directing me to Junior's sisters and allowing me to learn about Junior Hyde, my Uncle's friend.

Corporal Hubert Cothern another friend served in the army and was severely wounded after his unit entered the Battle of the Bulge in Belgium in late December 1944. He received multiple wounds in the chest and stomach sometime in late Janu-

Cpl. Hubert Cothern. Courtesy of the History of Mulhall, The First One Hundred Years.

ary or early February. His parents received word of his capture on February 5, 1945. He spent the rest of the war in Stalag 11 B at Fallingbostel as a Prisoner of War, guest of the German Government. Fallingbostel was located between Hamburg and Hanover. The experience in all prisoner of war camps was terrible, but Fallingbostel was one of the worst. Fallingbostel was designed to hold a few thousand troops, but by the end of the war more than 300,000 were kept there. Cpl. Cothern was liberated in April 1945 and returned to live in Mulhall for the rest of his long life.

There were others from the Mulhall community named in Uncle Wallace's letters, but I was not able to talk with them or their families. I am sure there were others not mentioned in the letters that served in the war. I have no knowledge of the things my Grandmother wrote to Uncle Wallace and she may have told of some, keeping him informed of the activities in the Mulhall community. The war had been over for sixty years before I started doing research and many were gone and with them went much history.

COUSINS AT WAR

During World War II there were many instances of family in uniform, father and son, brothers, brothers-in-law and many cousins. Wallace Dunn had several cousins who were in the war and served in different branches. Most he did not know, but they were at different times in the same battles or on the same ship transporting them to war. I have met and talked with a few and it has been interesting to learn of their experiences.

John Ray Lemons, a distant cousin, entered the service from Texas in January 1943. He and two friends applied for Cadet School with the Army Air Corps in 1942, but his application was rejected and he was told it was because of some surgery done in the past. He protested and supplied a copy of his medical records, along with a letter from his doctor. The information was sent to the Surgeon General for approval and Ray is still waiting for a reply. Ray later received a draft notice and went for induction. They ask him what branch of service he wanted and Ray replied. "The Air Corps does not want me. Any other will be all right." You guessed correctly, he was put in the Air Corps.

Ray's first training station was in Texas, followed by a time in Florida and then to Fort Meyers for gunnery school; then back to Texas for mechanics training. In November 1943, he went to Salt Lake City and was assigned to a crew and met the men whom he would serve with in Europe. They trained for the next several months and were given a fifteen day furlough. This was the usual procedure prior to being sent overseas. He returned from furlough and was stationed at Peterson Field in Colorado Springs. Ray enjoyed Colorado and wanted to live there after the war, but changed his mind.

Ray and his crew departed the States in June 1944 and sailed aboard the Queen Elizabeth, destination Europe. The Queen Elizabeth was a luxury passenger ship belonging to a British company. It had been redone and was used for troop transport during the war. The ship had 19,000 people on board, five hundred airmen, five hundred WAC's, with the others mostly Infantrymen. The airmen arrived last and had to take the worst accommodations. They were entertained by the Glenn Miller Band, which they enjoyed. Miller was not on board as he flew over. Sixty years later Ray discovered a cousin Kenneth Paul Dunn had been on the Queen Elizabeth also. They had never met and would not have known each other at the time. The ship docked at Gourock, Scotland.

Ray's crew flew in a B-24 Bomber, Piloted by James C. Baynham. The crew for the B-24 was four officers and six enlisted men. They were assigned to the 8th Air Force, 445th Bomb Group, 702nd Squadron stationed at Tibenham, near Norwich, England, located about ninety miles north of London.

Actor James Stewart was once the commanding officer of Tibenham, but had been promoted to Wing by the time Ray's crew arrived. Ray met a man who had been part of Stewart's crew. He told Ray, "We had great respect for Stewart as an officer and a pilot."

Stewart was not a desk man; he flew missions and accepted the danger with all the others.

Ray's normal position on the crew was waist gunner and assistant flight engineer. Shortly after he arrived at Tibenham, the ball turrets were removed from the planes requiring only a nine man crew. The men protested as they had trained together and wanted to fly missions together. This was allowed, but one man had to stay back on each mission, so they took turns.

The bombardier could not make the first mission and the pilot, who was always the plane commander, selected Ray as the Toggalier to drop the bombs. Ray dropped the bombs at the proper time in spite of heavy flak. Flak was the term used for shelling by the Germans from big guns on the ground. Many often described Flak as being so thick, one could walk on it. Ray was in the nose turret, where the bombardier sat to drop the bombs, when flak hit the turret blasting it sideways. The bullet proof glass was badly damaged and the navigator had to work hard to get the turret back in its normal position. Ray was not hurt, only shook up. They returned to base without any more problems. The Baynham Crew had been through their, "Baptism of Fire." They all thought the rest would be easy.

Mission three provided some excitement. The target was Dessau and on the bomb run their plane was flying last in the diamond formation with heavy flak. The plane to their right was hit and a wing fell off hitting a plane directly to their front. Both planes exploded, filling the air with debris and caused the Baynham plane to rollover and spin out of control, going down through the wreckage and causing their bombs to eject. All the men in the back of the plane had their chutes on and Ray tried to open the hatch for bail out, but the spinning plane and centrifugal force kept them pinned to the ceiling. The pilot and co-pilot worked frantically to get control of the plane, which they were able to do. They were now at low level, in a badly damaged plane, low on hydraulic fluid and did not know if the wheels, tires and brakes were all in good working order. They were also alone, separated from the others and in danger of being shot down by a German fighter plane, which often happened to a lone damaged plane. A single bomber was not capable of defending itself.

They made a slow return to base and were well behind the others on the mission. They flew over the base, dropping a flare and lined up for landing, which was almost perfect, much to their relief. The report was three planes lost that day over the target, not so as one was only a little late returning.

All members of the plane to the right, which was hit first, were killed. The other plane involved lost three killed and the others bailed out and were captured, spending the rest of the war in a German prison camp. Ray and his crew had survived another narrow escape, but there were more missions to come. The crews were to fly twenty five missions and then be relieved of combat flying. As the war progressed the number was raised to thirty five and some crews may have flown more than thirty five before the war ended. Flying with a bomber crew was dangerous and a large number were shot down during the war. The Air Corps was second to the Infantry in loss of personnel and equipment.

On September 27, 1944, Ray's crew flew their eighth mission. The target was the Henschel Munitions Works at Kassel, Germany. The 445th Group was to fly lead for the mission which consisted of 300 planes. Ray's Squadron started with thirty nine planes, but four had to drop out for various reasons. The weather was solid overcast for the entire day. The 445th made an incorrect navigational turn and communication between the groups questioned the route, but the 445th continued on their way, believing they were correct. The other planes did not follow and the 445th did not learn they had made an incorrect turn until years later. The 445th continued on and dropped their bombs on the secondary target, Gottingen, Germany.

After dropping their bombs the 445th was suddenly attacked by over one hundred German fighter FW-190 and ME-109's. The fifty caliber guns of the B-24's were no match against the fighter planes twenty and thirty caliber cannons and the fight was over quickly. Ray's plane, King Kong, was hit almost immediately and was on fire. Flames were coming through the bomb bay and back to Ray's position as a waist gunner. The parachutes for the waist gunners were kept near the bomb bay wall and Ray went to get them for himself and crew mate Olin Byrd. The tail gunner, John Knox who was seriously wounded crawled up to the waist gunner's position and was helped out of the plane. Byrd signaled Ray to go next and he jumped out pulling the rip cord on his chute immediately. The plane was at 23,500 feet altitude and pulling the cord that soon was the wrong thing to do. Clear thinking in this situation was not easy and one can understand his fear and anxiety. He was placed in a slow decent amid an air battle as some planes had exploded, were burning and the air was full of parachutes. One ME-109 was close enough for Ray to clearly see the pilot's face and Ray thought he was trying to dump his chute.

Ray had not properly adjusted his chute harness and when the chute opened he was nearly cut in half. He had been over confident and suffered some pain as a result. Ray soon became unconscious and fell for several thousand feet before regaining consciousness. He probably had passed out from the cold and lack of oxygen at the high altitude. The crews had to go on oxygen at 15,000 feet, when he fell below that point he regained consciousness. He was a little above the clouds, but shortly could see the ground and some trees and tried to guide away from them. After landing and removing the chute, he folded it and found a place to hide it. Ray had landed near the small town of Eisenach, Germany.

After a short walk, two farmers appeared with pitch forks and began jabbing at him. He tried to explain he was an American, but the Germans were angry at the Americans for bombing their towns and being American was no help at the moment. I believe the farmers were trying hard to kill him. Ray was saved by two very young German soldiers carrying long rifles with bayonets attached. They took control and moved him away from the angry farmers, shouting, Raus, Raus," which Ray thought meant for him to run. Running was difficult as he had on flying boots, his shoes were on the plane and he had not had time to change before bailing out. The German soldiers marched him to Eisenach, where other members of the 445th were gathered. Many were wounded from shrapnel or had burns.

On the way to Eisenach the group encountered a German official dressed in a fancy uniform wearing riding boots. The man was the Burgomaster of the small town and he stopped the group and began hitting some in the face with a pistol, screaming at them, calling them Chicago Gangsters, Terror Fleegers and other words Ray did not understand. Ray was on the front row and was being hit with the pistol. He tried to move away, but the man pointed the pistol at him and he decided running was the wrong thing to do and he had better stand and take the beating. The young soldiers again shouted, "Raus, Raus." The group all ran and soon saw about two dozen more members of the 445th Group. Most were in bad shape and the town of Eisenach had no medical help for them. They were put in the basement of a German Barracks and tried to care for the wounded during the night.

The next morning they were all marched to the train station, with those who could walk carrying the wounded on litters. As they proceeded to the train station, the local citizens shouted angry words, most of which they could not understand and they were again called Chicago Gangsters and Terror Fleegers. As Ray entered the station he looked across the tracks and saw five men hanging in their parachute shrouds. He was unable to determine if they were real or fake, but was probably put there to incite the local citizens.

After the war Ray learned about the other members of his crew. Bombardier Hector V. Scala, Navigator John W. Cowgill and radio Operator James T. Fields along with two other men from another crew were murdered after capture. Olin C Byrd, the other Waist Gunner was found dead and Ray does not know the circumstance of his death. John W. Knox, the Tail Gunner and Howard L. Boldt, the Flight Engineer/Gunner were both seriously wounded, but bailed out and both were captured, spending the rest of the war in Stalag Luft 1 at Barth. Pilot James C. Baynham and Co-Pilot Charles Bouquet, bailed out and were captured. They both spent the rest of the war in Stalag Luft 1 at Barth, Germany. Barth is on the Baltic Sea, about 100 miles from Berlin.

The train took Ray to an interrogation camp at Wetzlar, Germany, where he was questioned for three days. The process was exactly like the training films Ray had seen in the states. The only information he was to give was name, rank and serial number. Ray's interrogator offered him a Lucky Strike cigarette, which he did not accept and told him he had lived in Buffalo, New York before the war, but had returned to Germany in 1939. Ray was asked many questions, but continued to give only name, rank and serial number. Ray at first thought the man knew everything about his group, until he pulled out a book and told Ray, "You belong to the Johnson Crew." Ray ignored that statement; he was wrong.

After several days of confinement the group left Wetzlar on October 5th and went to Stalag Luft IV at Gross Tychow in northern Poland near the Baltic Sea. There were 10,000 POW's or Kreigies as they were called in the camp. There were four compounds in the camp and each room of the compound housed twenty five men. The men slept on wooden bunks with excelsior mattresses, had little food for the next two and one half months and very little clothing was furnished. Winter was coming and Ray had only the uniform he was wearing when captured, which was not sufficient for cold weather. The men received Red Cross parcels of food on occasion, which was meant for one man, but they were forced to share. The parcels along with Camp rations were not enough to sustain a person and all began losing weight. They had a cup, small spoon and knife to eat with. Enough food was always a problem and they devised a card game to fairly divide the food, which consisted of a bucket of soup, a small loaf of bread and a container of ersatz coffee. The soup was mostly water and contained little meat or vegetables. Only on Christmas Day 1944 did they get all of a special Red Cross parcel which had many goodies and Ray enjoyed every bite.

The camp had a secret system to receive broadcast from the BBC and they kept up with news of the war. In December 1944, during the Battle of the Bulge, the German guards told them they were winning, but they all knew the guards were lying because they had news from the BBC. Life was not easy; they did not have adequate toilet facilities or places to shower. Roll call was a daily routine and could be any time day or night. Ray had lots of time and he learned to knit, knitting a cap with ear flaps and has kept it all the years since the war. Each day was spent trying to stay warm and getting enough food.

The camp got notice the Russians were coming, which meant they would be moved to another camp. They knew the order to move would come at a moments notice and one day they heard artillery fire. They had saved food and other things to put in a towel, making a back pack. Early in the morning of January 31, 1945 they began the move with deep snow on the ground and temperatures about twenty degrees. German guards carrying rifles with bayonets attached and using dogs marched them several miles to a train station. They were then loaded in boxcars, about eighty men to a car, designed to hold forty men with no food or means of sanitation. The ride lasted for several days with no space to sit or lie down, conditions were terrible and many became sick with dysentery and other ailments. The train made stops to get water, but no food and they had to get by with what they had in their packs. Sanitation was a great problem and the situation was unbearable.

On February 8th the group arrived in Nuremberg and to Stalag XIII D which was overcrowded, lice infested, filthy and the food was the same. More POW's arrived daily and conditions grew worse. The prisoners broke the wood off the latrine wall and burned it to keep warm. The guards threatened to harm them if the person responsible did not confess. No person confessed and nothing happened. Ray watched each day for new arrivals, something to keep him busy and one day greeted his friend from Dallas, who had signed up for Cadets with him in 1942. He was a B-24 Pilot and Ray thought it was a small world after all. The British bombed Nuremberg several times at night and a bomb landed near the camp. The prisoners were in slit trenches, but Ray felt the bombs landed beside him. The prisoners were again notified they would have to move as the British and Americans were closing in on Nuremberg.

The Germans had POW camps scattered about Germany and as the Russians moved from the east and the Allies from the west they were running out of space and losing the war. Men from the camps were moved and most had to walk as the rail system in Germany had been bombed and they did not have fuel for trucks. The POW's feared the Germans would shoot them and not bother to make the move.

Beginning April 4th, Ray and about 2,000 others were forced to march in a column with only a few guards, traveling eighteen or twenty kilometers a day. They slept in farmer's barns or woods and with only a few guards were able to search for food buried around farms or trade D-Bars and cigarettes to the farmers for food. It was evident the war was about over as the roads were congested with AWOL German soldiers and displaced persons. One day the column was strafed by American P-47's. The pilots could see people on the road, but did not know they were American POW's. Ray was near the front of the column and he and a guard raced for protection of some trees. He was not hit, but some near the end of the column were injured. After the shooting stopped, Ray noticed the tree he and the guard were hiding behind was only about six inches thick, providing little protection. The guard had thrown his rifle away as they ran and he said to Ray, "Comrade nix goot." The POW's were able to trade for some bed sheets to use as markers and laid them out at each stop spelling POW. The planes stopped shelling them and only waved their wings as they flew over. They were able to learn of the death of President Roosevelt when marching through Holtshausen, Germany. They learned later Harry Truman was President and their new Commander-in-Chief. During the march they all received Swiss Red Cross packages which were like gifts from heaven. The reduced level of nutrition caused them to be unable to ward off sickness. They had few medical supplies, were exhausted and did not know when it would end.

After thirteen days of marching they arrived at Stalag VII A near Moosberg, Germany. It was April 13th and the war was about over, something they did not know. Ray had to endure fifteen more days in a POW camp. Conditions at Moosberg were not any different than the other camps. The camp had more than 100,000 POW's and was certainly not designed to handle that many. Ray's group had to live in tents, sleeping on the ground, food almost did not exist and the sanitary conditions were terrible. The day consisted of walking around looking for others Ray might know and trying to get food. American planes flew over the camp; usually P-51's and on one occasion they saw German ME-262 jets and wondered why they were so close. They soon learned General Patton's Armored Divisions were coming and that a battle for Moosberg was probable. They were told to not do anything stupid, stay down and out of harms way.

In the morning of April 29th, Ray could hear the noise of tanks and the shelling of Moosberg. The battle did not last long and tanks soon ran through the barbed wire fence surrounding the camp. One tank stopped near Ray and the tank commander opened the hatch and yelled, "Anyone from Texas?" Ray was standing less than forty feet away and replied, "Yes." The tanker then asks, "Where in Texas?" Ray said, "I am from Dallas." The tanker was also from Dallas and his name was Earl Cook. Ray had worked with his sister Ione. Ray told the tanker, "When you get home as you will beat me, please tell my folks you saw me and I am OK." Earl Cook was first to return home and visited Rays family telling them about Ray.

All the POW's went wild with emotion, excitement, tears and heart felt thanks at being free at last. It was the day they had all waited and prayed for and was finally a reality. Food, health care and clothing was made available and Ray's memory of the day is still with him. Things like white bread, something they had not seen in a long time was available once again.

Ray and a buddy decided to leave the camp and go to town, where they found a German family with a Hostel, Hotel, near the entrance of a bridge that crossed the Isar River. The bridge had been destroyed by the Germans, hoping to slow the advance of the Americans. When the German family learned Ray and his buddy were Americans, they welcomed them. The Germans did not want to be in the Russian zone of occupation and became friendly toward Americans. Ray and his buddy stayed at the Hostel until they were moved from Moosberg. The lady cooked meals for them and made some goodies, which

John Ray Lemons. Courtesy of Ray Lemons.

they enjoyed. They could not believe they had managed to hide that much food from the German authorities.

The war was still not over and Patton's tanks had to wait for the Engineers to build a new bridge and the tankers moved into the Hostel and found places to sleep. One day Gen. Patton came and was about three feet from Ray, reprimanding a Lieutenant for allowing his men to put sand bags on the tanks. He told the Lieutenant it cost extra fuel and slowed them down. The Lieutenant replied, "Yes Sir." The bags were quickly removed. With the bridge repaired the tankers moved on chasing the Germans for a few more days till the war was over on May 8, 1945.

On the day the war in Europe ended Ray was flown from Landshut, Germany to Rheims, France and by train went to Camp Lucky Strike in LaHarve. He was checked by the Medic's and was in his words fattened up. Ray said, "We ate till we couldn't." He left France on June 19th going to Fort Sam Houston, Texas and was home by the 27th, it was one happy day.

Ray was in three different prison camps, they were all different to some degree, yet much alike. Little food was given to him and what he did receive had to be divided among others. There was never enough and Ray was amazed at how thin a slice of bread could be. The Red Cross packages meant for one man had to be shared with another and only at Christmas was Ray able to enjoy one complete package. The Germans were out of food for their Army and food supply was very bad at the end of the war. Soup was served often and it was difficult to find any meat or vegetables, even a small piece of potato. Soup made from grains such as barley and was mostly water was common in the last days.

The Red Cross sent clothing, but the Germans did not give all of it to the prisoners. Most prisoners had only the clothes they wore when captured and one had to be lucky to get what they needed. The cold weather caused many to nearly freeze while waiting for the clothing issue and they suffered greatly when being marched through the snow.

The daily routine differed at each camp and at the last no routine could be depended on. Some days they received no food and all lost weight. Many died while in the camps from wounds not properly treated and others from dysentery and pneumonia.

Ray said, "We did get athletic equipment from the Red Cross, which was great, but we had to be very lucky after standing in line to find anything left at the issue point." The Red Cross also sent Bibles and books for the prisoners to read and Ray read over fifty of the books to make time pass faster. Playing cards also helped.

In each camp some group had access to the BBC and Ray was able to keep up with the war news. A Man of Confidence, who was their voice to the camp commander, was responsible for reading the news in each compound. The Germans never found out about the source of the BBC news.

Ray has been active in the 445th Bomb Group Association and the American Ex-POW Association attending reunions and other functions. He has been asked several times to attend to the details for the meetings and has everything ready when the others arrive. Ray's brother Curtis told me, "When they want something done, they call Ray."

Ray has returned to Europe at least two times to visit the place he was stationed and the farm on which he landed after bailing out of his plane. Tibenham Airfield has been maintained to some degree. The runways are intact and used today by the Norfolk Gliding Club. Part of the Headquarters building and a warehouse remain and the long runway used for take off and landings during the war is in good shape. A church at the end of the runway was used to line up for the landing. It is still there today and veterans have donated money to keep it in good condition. The steeple was an important part of the landscape and crews were happy to see it on their return from a mission.

During a visit to Tibenham in 1990, Ray and his wife Jean were invited, along with others stationed there during the war, to High Tea by some of the local citizens. Ray and Jean went to the home of a man who as an eight year old boy often visited the base during the war. He told them he was given food served in a tin cup, which was the issued mess kit for all servicemen. The man now has a home on land that was part of Tibenham during the war. The couples have become friends, visiting in each others homes.

On the same trip in 1990 while in Germany Ray met a German couple who have become interested in the war and do research on downed planes. Using memory of forty five years from the past, Ray drew a map of the area where he landed after bailing out. The couple used the map and found the farm and Ray went to see it on another visit in 2006. The farm has been abandoned and the roads relocated, but Ray thinks it is the correct place.

Ray has many friends that were at Tibenham during the war and they stay in touch by phone and reunions. Those friendships are still important after more than sixty years. The Co-Pilot, Charles Bousquet never attended a reunion or made contact with any member of the crew after the war and the only information they have about him is that he died in 1956.

In early September 1944, the 3rd Army ran out of supplies near Metz, France. Ray remembers he and his crew flew gasoline in five gallon cans loaded in the bomb bay of the B-24 to a temporary landing site near Nancy, France to resupply the 3rd Army. One time it was medical supplies. The trips were called trolley missions and were not counted as combat missions. Ray and Cousin Wallace Dunn were very close together at this time, but did not know it.

The bombing of Pearl Harbor on December 7, 1941 got the attention of Americans and Ray and his friends were no exception. They were angry and discussed the possibility of war to come and how they could be a part of it. Ray felt it was his duty to be involved and he and two of his friends volunteered as Cadets in the Air Corps. He believes fighting World War II was the right thing to do.

Another cousin of Wallace Dunn was Rex O. Brannon. He was born in Texas May 18, 1920. He spent most of his life in or around Bay City. Rex was inducted in the service on April 7, 1943, was not married and had grown up during the great depression of the late 1920's and 30's. The tough time of the depression had conditioned most American youth to live simply. They were not used to much luxury and Army life did not provide anything different.

Rex went to Camp Gruber in Oklahoma for training. Camp Gruber was located near the small town of Braggs, twenty miles south of Muskogee. Rex became a member of the 42nd Infantry Division. This division had fought in World War I and was named the Rainbow Division because its members came from all parts of the United States, thus they covered the states like a rainbow. Rex would be in the 222nd Regiment, I Company until March 1945. He was transferred to K Company, probably to give the Company an experienced man when they received replacements due to battle casualties.

The 222nd Regiment left Camp Gruber on November 13, 1944 and went by train to Camp Kilmer, New Jersey. They received new equipment and practiced beach landings from a ship. The censoring of their mail began at this time. All Regiments of the 42nd boarded the USAT Edmund B. Alexander and were bound for Europe by the 25th. The Regiments were the 222nd, 232nd and the 242nd. Not all of the 42nd Division left at this time as the headquarters and others remained in the states; the assistant commander of the division, Brigadier General Henning Linden, was in command. The Unit was called

Sgt. Rex Brannon. Courtesy of Jack Brannon.

By Melvin Dick / 119

Task Force Linden and would remain under Gen. Linden until February 1945 after the rest of the Division joined them.

The task force arrived in Marseille, France and disembarked on December 8, 1944. The next day was spent in getting tents set up and of course they had to be in perfect alignment. During the night of the 8th a German plane came over and dropped a few bombs, not doing much damage, and they learned tents in perfect rows made a good target. The next day was spent moving the tents to irregular positions and digging slit trenches. Task Force Linden was a green unit in the war and had a lot to learn. After receiving more equipment, clothing and taking showers they were ready to move on. All Regiments were loaded on 40 and 8 box cars, a term from World War I, meaning the cars loaded would hold 40 Humans or 8 Horses, on the 18th and went by train to Bensdorf, near Strasbourg, France. On the 24th, Christmas eve Rex was introduced to the war.

Rex wrote about his first time in battle. He was picked to go on patrol and was instructed to make contact with the enemy. The mission was accomplished and the patrol was able to return without casualties. The patrol had been simple enough and the Rex thought being on patrol was not bad. The next day he was again picked for another patrol. The mission was to locate enemy Artillery positions. They had to move at least five miles out into no mans land, which put them a long way from any help or protection from the rest of the Regiment. Rex along with fourteen others made their way up the side of a long hill. To the left were trees and to the right open country. They observed some German soldiers cutting wood near a house. The Sergeant told them to get ready and fire on his command. The Sergeant yelled," Fire" and the soldiers ran for cover, with rifle fire they were able to kill and wound some of the enemy. Three men had been left behind as a rear guard and when they heard the shooting, quickly returned to the unit and reported the patrol had been fired on and they thought some were killed and others wounded. They apparently did not try to find out what had happened.

As they were close to a small village, the Sergeant ordered them to fire three mortar rounds. The patrol fired the mortar and the first round went off, but landed about one hundred and fifty feet to the front. Something was wrong and they discovered ice in the mortar tube. They used a bayonet to clear the ice and fired the other two rounds on target. The patrol then returned to their unit. On the way they met some Medics carrying stretchers. The Medics had reacted to the report of the rear guard and were going to help the patrol. Two patrols and no casualties were rare in the war and Rex was happy to be back with the others.

Rex and the 222nd moved twenty miles to Blasheim, southwest of Strasbourg. Trucks were to be available, but none arrived and the Regiment had to walk. They started with full packs, but were not able to finish the march carrying the heavy packs. They threw away everything except weapons, ammunition, food and blankets. They relieved elements of the 36th Infantry Division. At this time several men were transferred to the 90th Infantry Division, leaving them short of the original number and they would not be at full strength for the rest of the war.

The Regiment was placed in a valley, high hills on both sides with the enemy looking down on them. This would seem to be a foolish thing to do. They began digging foxholes and cut logs to place over the top which was a great help when they received Artillery fire. The Germans soon started shelling them.

The Company Command Post was in a house and not far from Rex's foxhole. The Company Commander, a Second Lieutenant and his radio operator were inside. The Lieutenant spotted a German patrol and ordered a machine gunner to shoot them, but they were too far away. The Germans maneuvered until they had Rex and his unit in machine gun crossfire. One man was killed and several wounded. One wounded man had to wait for darkness before the medics could go help him.

The next day Artillery shelling was intense. A shell hit the CP and the Lieutenant ran out and got in a foxhole. The shelling continued through the night, hitting close to Rex's foxhole, causing him and his buddy to cross the road to another hole. This was a good move as the first foxhole received a direct hit. When the shelling stopped, Rex counted twelve hits close to his old foxhole, plus the direct hit. The next morning hot food was brought to them by a Jeep. The enemy spotted the Jeep and fired several rounds, killing one man and wounding others. During a time of constant shelling, one man would go get food for both. The company kitchens tried to feed the men hot food at least once a day. Food was brought to the front by Jeep, pulling a small trailer. The Germans knew this was the practice and would watch for the Jeep. When the men began to expose themselves, the shelling would start. It was a cat and mouse game.

Rex remembered on a dark night, they would set traps by tying grenades to a wire and hang them between trees. This served as a warning of enemy patrols. In one instance a horse tripped the grenade and the shooting started. Rex did not say what happened to the horse.

During a German counterattack, the unit machine guns fired most of the night. The next morning revealed eight wounded enemy soldiers in front of the foxholes. The soldiers were almost frozen due to very cold weather. Rex's foxhole buddy wanted to shoot them, but Rex refused to let him. They had to drag the soldiers on the snow to the aid station for treatment. Soon after fifty Germans came out and surrendered.

The lieutenant had been in the foxhole too long, not moving and on his knees. The temperature was below freezing. When they lifted him out he was unable to walk and had to be carried from the battlefield.

The 101st Airborne Division relived the 222nd on January 27th. They were sent to Luneville to rest and receive replacements. They stayed there until February 12, were fed well and watched it snow for several days. Men were shifted to give the Platoons experienced people and help train the replacements. Awards were given and Rex having been under enemy shelling for at least thirty days was awarded the Combat Infantry Badge. The rest of the Division had arrived and joined them. The 42nd Division was together again and Task Force Linden was no more.

The 222nd was sent to relieve elements of the 45th Infantry Division on February 16th. Company K relieved Company K of the 179th Regiment. The mission was to crack the West Wall or the Siegfried Line. They spent thirty days in the vicinity of Althorn along the Moder River.

Rex was moved from I Company on March 2, 1945 to K Company, where he would remain until he went home after the war. Battle casualties often demanded men with combat experience be moved to another Platoon or Company to fill important vacancies. The 222nd fought through the West Wall and crossed the Rhine River at Worms on March 31, 1945. They passed near Heidelberg, going to Miltenburg, Germany.

The 42nd Division arrived at the Dachau Concentration Camp at 0630 hours May 1. They witnessed a terrible sight. Rex saw rail cars full of Jews that had been starved to death. The cars contained men, women and children. Others in the camp were barely alive showing signs of brutal treatment. Never in the history of man have there been any other scene of such horrendous treatment of humans. Army Signal Corps members took photographs. General Dwight Eisenhower, The Allied Supreme Commander for the European Theater, ordered each Division to send as many soldiers as possible to be a witness. Senators and Representatives from the United States also came. General Eisenhower wanted as many as possible to witness the event as he felt such things would one day be denied. He was correct.

Rex Brannon died August 31, 1990. His eldest son Jack found in his wallet a picture of the dead in a boxcar. An Army photographer had given it to him and he carried it every day for the rest of his life. The photo is faded and worn, but there can be no mistake about the figures in the photo.

During the war Rex killed twenty six men that he knew about. This bothered him all his life. We can only speculate as to why he carried the photo. Perhaps it was to justify the twenty six men he killed. Maybe it was a reminder of why the war was necessary or he may have used it as evidence for those who said such things did not happen. I am sure he could never forget the sight at Dachau. He had a reason to do his part to maintain freedom in the world, especially for his children and grandchildren.

After the war was over in May 1945, the 42nd served as occupation troops in Germany until June 11 when they were moved to Austria. They finally were stationed in Vienna by early August. They had to cross through the Russian zone of occupation. On August 8th, Company K arrived in a rainstorm with 243 Enlisted Men and 10 Officers. They were billeted in a large mansion with plumbing and electric power working. It was probably the best living quarters of any time during the war. Rex was the Mess Sergeant for his company. After feeding the troops each day Rex gave the local citizens anything left over. A local Doctor and his wife knew Rex did this and after the war wrote to him asking for care packages.

During the time Rex was in Vienna, he met a lady with a two year old boy. They wrote letters to each other for a few years after the war. Some years later, Rex eldest son Jack was in College and met another student whose father was working in the American Embassy in Vienna. Jack told him about his father being station in Vienna during the war and about the lady with the young son. One day the guy told Jack he was going to Vienna to visit his father. Jack made copies of the pictures of the lady and her son, along with copies of some of the letters his father had received. Three years later Jack got a phone call from the lady's son. He was surprised, but delighted. The friendship has lasted for years as they write and keep in touch.

Sergeant Rex Brannon came home from the war and his relatives and friends remarked how he had changed. He married and had a family. Rex also maintained contact with his buddies from the war and helped those living near him. He took several to Veterans Hospitals for treatment, but never used the Veterans Hospital himself. His son Jack does not know the reason.

Tom Brannon, a cousin from Tennessee entered the service November 7, 1941, exactly one month before the bombing of Pearl Harbor. He did basic training at Ft. Bragg, North Carolina and then went to radio school at Ft. Knox, Kentucky. Tom was assigned to the 2nd Armored Division and did many months of training with them, taking part in the war games known as the Tennessee Maneuvers. In late 1942, Tom left New York on a troop ship that took him to North Africa landing at Casablanca, Morocco. Tom's oldest brother was a Combat Engineer and he saw him at Casablanca and was able to spend one evening with him. They planned to meet the next day, but his brother could not get off duty. The 2nd Armored moved out during the day and they did not see each other until the end of the war. Tom was a part of the assault landing on Sicily in July 1943. Anyone reading about General George Patton will know he landed at Gela and Tom was there. Tom wrote his brother a letter telling him he was at Sicily. His brother had been angry because his Lieutenant would not let him off to visit with Tom. After finding out Tom was in Sicily, he told the Lieutenant, "If my brother is killed in this war and I am not, I am going to stick this Tommy gun up your nose and hold the trigger until it runs out of shells." Tom said, "My brother could be a hard man at times."

Sicily was the first use of American airborne troops during the war and they had a bad experience. The Navy was told of the arrival of airborne forces during the night and they were not to fire on them. Not everyone got the message and when the planes bringing them arrived, one gun fired and the others followed killing and wounding a large number by downing the planes and shooting the men as they descended in their chutes. Tom witnessed the sad event. He remembered seeing the troops hanging from trees the next morning. Most were dead with only a few badly wounded. The killing or wounding of troops by friendly fire happened in World War II and has occurred in all the wars since.

In the movie, PATTON, there is scene from the war in Sicily when Gen. Patton shot two mules on a bridge, then had some men throw them off into the river, because they were holding up the movement of the troops. Tom was not far from this scene and knew it did happen. The Sicily Campaign lasted only about six weeks. It did not take the Allies long to drive the enemy off the Island,

After Sicily the 2nd Armored Division went to England for more training to get ready for the Normandy invasion. They arrived in England, by ship the day before Thanksgiving in 1943.

Tom and the 2nd Armored Division landed on Omaha Beach on D + 4 or June 10, 1944. Tom remembers seeing a large number of ships in the channel bringing more troops and supplies. The ships were one behind the other, lined up, waiting to drop the troops or supplies. The war had not moved far from the beach and the scene was horrific. Destroyed ships, tanks and vehicles of all kinds were in the water along the beach. The Graves Registry Units were transporting bodies for burial. The wounded were being loaded on ships returning to England.

One of Tom's stories about Normandy involved Artillery shelling. Tom remembered that they always had a halftrack to carry the radio equipment and when artillery fire came they would get under the halftrack until it stopped. Normandy was farm country and there were many cows and where there are cows there will also be cow manure. On one occasion during artillery fire by the enemy, Tom and his comrades made a dash for the halftrack. Tom dived under the halftrack sliding through a cow pile. It went inside his shirt and when the shelling stopped he tried to wipe the shirt clean on the grass, but was not successful. Tom noticed no one sat by him during chow for the next two days. He was finally able to find enough water to wash the shirt.

The fighting continued to move inland and the 2nd Armored did their part to help. There would be hard fighting and dangerous times for Tom as they moved across France and into Belgium. Tom remembered the German buzz bombs flying over Belgium, most on their way to England. Some of the buzz bombs did hit Belgium. The bombs had enough fuel for a certain distance and then the motor that drove them would sputter and they dropped to earth. They were capable of destroying a city block and Tom was quick to find a foxhole when he heard the sputtering sound. After the Battle of The Bulge, the 2nd Armored fought to the Rhine River and made the crossing, putting them well into Germany.

Another memory of Tom's was the story about an American C-47 and a German ME-109 fighter plane. The C-47 was the workhorse of the war, hauling not only troops, but supplies. An unescorted C-47 was flying in Germany one day when a ME-109 happened to see it. The enemy pilot played with the C-47, flying under and above and faking a head on crash. The pilot of the ME-109 knew the C-47 was an unarmed American plane and was probably going to end the game and shoot it down. On one pass by the ME-109 a man in the back of the C-47 shot at the pilot with a rifle and killed him. This was an unusual thing and not expected. The man received the Air Medal for his action that day.

The 2nd Armored Division was chosen as the occupation force of Berlin after the war ended and they arrived there on July 4, 1945. The Russians had captured Berlin and they were everywhere. It was a difficult job maintaining order in that situation.

The 2nd Armored Division was privileged to be entertained three times by members of the USO. Tom saw Bob Hope all three times and enjoyed the shows.

Tom was discharged September 30, 1945 and was back home by October 10th, feeling fortunate to have survived the war. He had been many places and seen more than his share of fighting in almost four years of service time. Tom had a good sense of humor and related stories of times with his buddies when on pass. He had a buddy that always could get him in some trouble. Tom never could think of a way to get back, until one night in London during blackout and they were going down the street following some English girls. Tom walked beside one of the girls and reached back and patted her on the behind. He did it more than once before she became angry and turned around and slapped his buddy. The man got the slapping a couple more times before he figured out Tom was causing it. He told Tom, "You do that again and I am going to give you a good beating." Tom knew he could make good the threat and never did it again, but he did get him back at least once. Tom must have read a lot of books on the war and was always telling of being there or nearby when things happened that was written about in the books. Two family members recorded his memories of the war and wrote the story leaving for them a record of Tom's service in World War II.

At this writing Tom is doing well for a man ninety years old. He is a pleasure to talk with and I found him to be like many other Veterans of the war, remembering many of his experiences. He was most gracious in giving me permission to write some about his war time experiences.

Another cousin, Ralph Dunn, from Waldron, Arkansas, enlisted in the Coast Guard on November 20, 1942. He did the usual stateside training before being shipped overseas aboard the USS Kirkpatrick, a Destroyer Escort. The ship was not large being only 305 foot long and 35 foot wide. There were usually thirty five to forty ships in each convoy. The first destination was the Straits of Gibraltar in 1943. A Destroyer was used to guard large ships carrying men and equipment or supplies. Ralph was to make thirty crossing during the war. Other than the enemy Ralph experienced flying fish and whales. They were always on the lookout for floating mines and enemy submarines. Ralph spent many days and nights as a lookout on deck exposed to the weather, that at times was very cold and on some days raining.

Life aboard ship was boring as well as exciting. During storms that had waves large enough to capsize the ship, Ralph remembers thinking the ship would break apart or roll over and sink. On one occasion at night the ship was suddenly illuminated by a bright light that only lasted for a few seconds. They learned it was from a B-25 Bomber on patrol looking for enemy submarines and they had turned on the light to check the ship and determine what country it belonged to. During rough weather, talking a shower would often turn out to be a beating, because he could not shower and stay on his feet on the wet shower floor. He may have decided against a shower during rough seas.

One time when the ship was in Port, a ham from the kitchen was missing. The Captain told the men there would be no liberty until the ham was found. The ham was to be put by the door of the Captain's quarters and no questions would be asked. The ham quickly appeared, because the men valued their liberty.

Ralph was married when he enlisted and his wife managed to be with him at times during training, but she like many other wives had to wait out each day praying their husbands were going to return and the war would quickly end. The end came on October 4, 1945 for Ralph and he was home at last. He used the GI Bill to attend College, getting a degree in Pharmacy. Many years after the war Ralph decided to write about his experiences and has left a very detailed story.

Kenneth Paul Dunn is a cousin most closely related to Uncle Wallace. He has a great memory of the war and can tell many stories of his experiences. His recall of dates, places and happenings as well the men whom he knew during the war is fantastic after more than sixty five years.

Ken was born in the new hospital in Kingsville, Texas on October 14, 1920. His growing up years was typical of the time. After graduating from high school, Ken worked for a civil engineering company from the fall of 1939 to November 1940 when he joined the National Guard. The work took them to the King Ranch to survey boundaries and locations for building sites. It was rugged work walking all parts of the ranch and may have conditioned Ken for life in the Army.

On November 23, 1940, Ken joined the Texas National Guard, the 36th Infantry Division. He was a member of Battery F, 2nd Battalion, 133rd Field Artillery Regiment and the 61st Artillery Brigade, a 155mm Howitzer unit. The Texas National Guard, like all of the other states guard divisions was ordered to federal service for one year. That one year of duty turned into five years because after the bombing of Pearl Harbor, the United States declared war against Japan on December 8, 1941.

Ken began duty at home station on November 25, 1940 and he reported at 0630 hours in a uniform that was not complete and most of it did not fit. His unit was stationed at the Kingsville Fairgrounds and he lived in a livestock feeding barn. One day he was put on KP and in the evening was called to the battery command post for guard detail. He had to quickly learn the Ten General Orders, was then issued a rifle and walked his post for four hours. When coming off guard duty he saw a man who knew he had also been on KP that same day. He was told it was a serious violation of Army Regulations to be ordered to do KP and Guard Duty on the same day and he should report the violation immediately. The Battery Commander, First Sergeant and Clerk listened carefully as all three had been involved. The Commander asks if he felt well enough to walk a second shift, which he did. The result was that he was never ordered to do KP again. After about three weeks Battery F was sent to a new station being built at Camp Bowie, Texas.

Ken trained for about five weeks as a cannoneer and was moved to the Howitzer section after which he was assigned different jobs helping the unit to get organized. He then settled down to learn mathematics and procedures of the Instrument Corporal and the duties of Instrument Sergeant and Battery Reconnaissance Officer. All was normal preparation for wartime losses.

After wearing out the mix of uniforms he started with, new uniforms began arriving and he was issued clothing of good quality that fit. The Army had not been ready for the great influx of men in 1940 and it took some time for all to receive proper uniforms and equipment.

Ken attended the Artillery Officers Candidate Course at Fort Sill, Oklahoma, graduating first in his class and was commissioned a 2nd Lieutenant on August 1, 1942. He then stayed at Fort Sill as an instructor in the Field Artillery Gunnery School and six months later was promoted to 1st Lieutenant. He then taught an Officer Course with students ranked from 1st Lt. to Lt. Col.

After going through maneuvers in Tennessee, his unit was moved to Tullahoma and began preparing for overseas shipment. The Howitzers were sent by rail to a port and loaded on a ship and arrived in England before the troops. In early June 1944, Ken's unit boarded the Queen Elizabeth in New York on their way to England. The Queen Elizabeth was a luxury liner that had been converted to accommodate troops being sent to Europe. The Queen Elizabeth was the largest and fastest ship of the time and could have made the trip in two days. Because of the threat of sinking by German Submarines, the ship had to navigate an irregular course and the trip took six days. Ken tried for about one half day to determine the navigational pattern. He could not find any time or speed that was the same.

On one occasion when Ken was officer of the guard, he was charged with preparing a barricade to keep male and females apart as there were some members of the Women's Army Corps on board next to them on the same deck. As he was preparing the barricade, he noticed one of the WAC's watching with great interest. She said with a smile, "that won't stop me." Ken replied, "It won't keep me out either." He then made a serious barricade which must have proved satisfactory as he did not report any problems.

The Glenn Miller Band was on board and they played for

the troops, something all enjoyed. Glenn Miller was not on the ship as he had flown across. Also on board was Ray Lemons, a distant cousin. Ken and Ray learned of this about sixty years later. The Queen Elizabeth docked in Greenock, Scotland and all went ashore listening to Scotsmen in kilts, playing bagpipes and drums.

Ken had been assigned to the 740th Artillery Battalion and was at this time in S-2, Intelligence and Reconnaissance, of the heavy Artillery Battalion. They were able to get their Howitzers, but an English Supply Depot sent them ammunition for a British eight inch gun and it was useless to the Americans. They were quickly able to remedy the situation.

The 740th landed on Utah beach August 10, 1944. They moved through the hedgerow country and turned south toward Brest. Ken's duty at this time was to do a personal reconnaissance of the terrain and troop concentrations, both enemy and Allied and report what he found to Headquarters. If a target of opportunity was observed he could call for Artillery fire and try to eliminate the target. The fighting to capture Brest was over by September 19th and the 740th then moved across France to Belgium, arriving there on October 3rd.

When the Battle of The Bulge began Ken had been promoted to Captain and was commanding Battery A of the 740th and his Battery was positioned north of Prum, Germany at the north end of the Schnee Eifel. On the morning of December 16, Ken was awakened by the sound of a Buzz Bomb. He had not heard a bomb go over for about three weeks and instantly knew something big was about to happen. The 106th Infantry Division's Artillery was close to him. The 106th had recently arrived in Germany and had not seen any combat. They had been placed in their present position, thought to be a quiet sector for training. The German attack hit elements of the 106th Infantry units and they were quickly overrun sustaining heavy causalities and entire Company's were captured.

Higher Headquarters had ordered units in the area to spend eight hours a day building log cabins presumed to be for winter quarters for the men in the area. This was a big mistake as morale instantly declined as the men suspected a long war. Ken felt it was a mistake for at least two reasons, the units would not have time to train or do any maintenance of their equipment. No time to train may have been at least part of the reason the 106th was not prepared.

Battery A was ordered out of the area and had to do a slow move, because of heavy military traffic, to a position near Sedan, France, south of the Meuse River. They remained in that position until the middle of January 1945. After the bulge had been eliminated, the Allies went on the attack and began pushing the Germany Army back over the German border. The 740th had more firing missions as the war carried them over the Rhine River well into Germany by April, 1945. Ken was wounded near Greiz, Germany on April 16, 1945 and was in the hospital recovering when the war ended.

In 1959 Ken was a Major, stationed at Fort Sam Houston,

Major Ken Dunn [Courtesy of Ken Dunn]

Texas. He participated in the All-Army Pistol Shooting match at Fort Benning, Georgia and became the Army's Individual Pistol Champion. In late 1958 to January 1962, Ken was the Officer in Charge of the 4th Army Advanced Marksmanship Detachment at Fort Sam Houston. We did not know at the time, but Ken and I were both at Fort Sam Houston in 1960.

In 1966 as Ken was finishing a three year tour on the faculty at The Command and General Staff College, located at Fort Leavenworth, Kansas, he received a letter from the Chief of Military History. He was asked to go to Vietnam as Command Historian for the US Army Vietnam, which he accepted. While at Fort McNair, Virginia to learn the details of the assignment, he met Lt. Col. Charles MacDonald, The Deputy Chief and over the next several months they became good friends. Lt. Col. MacDonald was a veteran of World War II and wrote a few books about the war. My favorites are, Company Commander and A Time for Trumpets. He also helped to write the History of World War II, which is in several books and became known as The Green Books, because of their color.

Ken went to Vietnam and through his efforts, new polices were established. He was not writing history, but was able to insure for the future, an adequate documentary basis in every Army Unit Command so the best original source documents would be available to historians, even those writing decades after the events.

Ken is ninety years old and lives alone, but does restrict involvement in some activities. Through Ken's writings I have gained some insight into the workings of a heavy artillery unit in World War II. Ken's time in the Army along with his detailed memory would make an interesting book. The things I have written about him only scratch the surface of his interesting life.

There were of course other cousins in the war, but I don't have their stories. They and their memories are gone and most may have never recorded for their families the experience that most could not completely forget. It was almost impossible for all serving during the war to not have other family members also serving.

12

AFTERWORD

The war was over and those who served began arriving back in the States in record numbers. Most had dreamed of returning home and back to life as it had been before the war. It seemed simple enough, but in reality it was not. Those who were front line soldiers and had been under stress from shell fire and living conditions that were unimaginable, could not simply turn off the war. They experienced nightmares, reliving the sights of the war and found they could not sleep all night and would wake up in panic because they could not find their constant companion, the rifle. During the war most did not have the luxury of sleeping in houses, in beds and they could not quickly return to normal. They missed the company of the men they had served with because they felt they were the only ones that understood them. Some have commented they wanted to go back and be with their Army buddies. They did not want war, just wanted to be with those who understood.

Many could not return to normal and life was usually short and terrible for them. The memories of buddies being killed or severely wounded within two or three feet from them, or the terrible times under artillery fire was something they could not put out of their mind. Most were able to overcome the memories of the war and move on. It was not quick and easy, but with the help of family and friends they managed to adjust to civilian life. The war had changed the men and the entire world. The GI Bill was available for education and thousands took advantage of the aid in money to attend a College or University. Many became teachers and found teaching satisfying because they were building and not destroying as they had done in the war.

I would guess the United States set a record for marriages in the first year following the war. This caused increased needs for housing and new jobs were created as housing additions was added in every State. Along with the record marriages came record numbers of babies and those born at this time have been known as Baby Boomers. The increase in family numbers caused the need for everything to sustain life. Auto makers began producing cars in record numbers; medical faculties sprang up, grocery stores, clothing stores and furniture stores to furnish all the new homes, causing the United States to produce more goods and services than the world had ever known. Hard surfaced roads were built to handle all the traffic and travel became quick and easy. Air travel became popular as the war had produced reliable planes and pilots and the world became smaller. Telephone and electric service soon was common in the rural areas of the country making work faster and easier.

Technology brought new and exciting things from medicine to toilet paper. The veterans caused most of this to happen as they had experienced during the war what working together could produce. The veterans had definite ideas about how things should be done and they took charge.

The veterans were present everywhere in my life. They were my teachers in high school and college. They lived next door or just down the street and were leaders in my church and where I worked. Most did not talk about the war to their families until much later in life. They talked to veterans, but were reluctant to talk with others. They will not say much today unless they think you understand. I recently asked one about medals he received. His reply was, "I usually don't talk about that, but will tell you because I think you understand." All of the men from World War II have been very helpful and most gracious to me over the years and have come to treat me as one of their own. I feel special and humble. They have helped me to understand the people involved in World War II. The men from the 10th Infantry Regiment will always have a special place in my heart and I will never forget them and what they did for me and the world.

The men of the 10th accomplished much in the war, yet for

as great as they were, very few found any glory in war. They did not fight for Country, Flag and Patriotism, but more because it was the right thing to do. They fought to keep themselves and their buddies alive and as they moved across Europe the effect of an oppressed people was evident. Those who liberated one of the Concentration Camps quickly understood what they were fighting for and against. They fought to preserve freedom, theirs, mine and yours.

It has been a great honor to talk with the men of the 10th Regiment and record their story. Time is quickly taking them and soon none will be left to give us the real story of the war. I feel privileged to have known them and had the opportunity to get first hand their story before they and their memories fade.

ACKNOWLEDGEMENTS

The writing of a book requires a lot of help from various sources. Without the help and encouragement of many people it would not have been possible to write the story. I cannot find adequate words to express my appreciation to the men of the 10th Regiment, who made their memories available to me. My sincere thanks to Ralph Cupelli, Jack Davis, Frank Langfitt, Byron Liebner, Harold Storey and Tom Tucker for stories and photos. Thanks to Earl Waldron for the list of names and addresses, that made it possible for me to find the men of C Company.

Thanks to Brad Clover for telling me about his father and providing photos. Sandra MacDuffee was my first contact concerning the 10th Regiment and has provided the story about her father Pfc. John Chichilla, along with photos of her trips to Luxembourg and her kindness for sending me a map of Luxembourg.

My appreciation to cousin Jack Brannon for the story about his father Rex Brannon, to cousins Ray Lemons and Ken Dunn for their story of World War II and also cousin Tom Brannon for allowing me to quote from his account of the war.

Thanks to Roy and Ann McNeill for guiding me through the history of Mulhall and to Rachel Stephenson for stories of men in the war from Mulhall. Thanks to Blanche Hill for the story of her brother and to Wayne Murphy and Margie Anthis for their memories of Wallace Dunn. Thanks also to my Aunt, the late Faye Hunt for memories of her brother Wallace Dunn.

Keith Short, the National Historian of the Society of The Fifth Division also provided information about the men of the 5th Division in World War II. Keith was more than willing to help and encouraged me to do research and write about the 5th Division men who fought the war.

Lois Hicks, my next door neighbor did excellent work on the many photos to make them the best they could be. She spent many hours working with the photos and her help is much appreciated.

I cannot find adequate words to thank JoAnn Phillips, a Published Author and writer of several books, for her help with the manuscript and encouraging me to keep going. From the beginning JoAnn believed the story should be told and gave me needed help with my writing skills.

My thanks and appreciation to Douglas Dollar of The New Forums Press for taking the book and his guidance and patience with this first time author.

My sisters, Joyce Huffer, Rose Marie McDaniel and Doris Beecham deserve my appreciation for reading the final manuscript and correcting spelling, punctuation and typos. They had the assistance of sister-in-law Bobbie Lemons, and that made it a family affair.

Thanks to my friend and golfing partner, Richard Dally for keeping my computer going. His understanding of the monster is way beyond anything I will ever accomplish.

My love and appreciation to my daughter Shelly for helping me with my computer and telling me, "Dad you can do it."

My wife Treva was the first to suggest that I should write about my Uncle Wallace Dunn. I have been a student of World War II for more than thirty years, but had not attempted to write about the war. I had one course in college that required some writing, but that has been more than fifty years in the past. Treva read all the chapters, some more than once and made suggestions to improve my effort. She lived with me and the 5th Division for more than five years and I appreciate her time and encouragement.

```
KM W Ck 49 Govt
WUX Washington D.C. 1013PM Feb 17th 1945
Mrs Mary A Dunn Route 1
Orlando, Okla.

The Secretary of War asks that I assure you of his deep sympathy
in the loss of your Son Private First Class Melvin W. Dunn who
was previously reported missing in Action. Report now received
states he was killed in Action Twenty Eight January in Luxembourg
Comfirming  letter follows.

            J.A. Ulio the Adjustant General
            745AM Feb 19th 1945.
```

SOURCES

Books

Ambrose, Stephen E. *D-Day June 6, 1944: The Climatic Battle of World War II*, Simon & Schuster, 1994.

Colley, David P. *Safely Rest.* Caliber, Penguin Group [USA], 2004.

D'Este, Carlo. *Decision in Normandy.* HarperCollins, 1983.

Hechler, Ken. *The Bridge at Remagen.* Pictorial Histories Publishing Company, 1995.

Histories

Public Relations Section, *Tenth Infantry Regiment. A Combat Narrative, History of the Tenth Infantry Regiment, Military Service Company*, 1946.

The Fifth Division Historical Section, Headquarters Fifth Infantry Division. *The Fifth Infantry Division in the ETO.* The Battery Press Inc, Reprinted 1997.

INDEX

A
Allen, Pat 101- 102
Anthis, Margie 6
Arnaville, 16, 23, 30, 55-56
Ardennes, 65-66
Arry, 57-58

B
Battle of the Bulge, 1, 17, 28, 31
Baynaham, James C. 107, 111
Beehive Jack, 60
Belfast, 14
Bell, Robert 13, 18, 48, 90
Bolt, Howard 111
Bomb Group 445th, 107, 109-110, 117
Booby trap, 47, 52
Bouquet, Charles 111, 118
Bradley, Omar 47, 67, 70
Brannon, Jack 124-125
Brannon, Rex 118-124
Brannon, Tom 124-127
Breckinridge, William 13, 48
Bronze Star, 25
Brown, Robert 58
Burgett, Donald 70-71
Byrd, Olin 109, 111

C
Campbell, A.B. 70
Camps, Abbott, 28 Bowie, 129
  Campbell, 92 Fannin, 99 Gruber, 119 Kilmer, 93, 119 McCain, 8-9 Shanks, 9, 29, 92
Cassells, Robert W. 71-72
Chichilla, John 59, 92, 96-97
Churchill, Winston 35, 40, 79
Clover, Brad 97, 100
Clover, Homer 99-100
Clover, Phil 99
Clover, Phillip 58, 79, 98-100
Company C 2, 10, 16-19, 23-27, 30, 46, 48, 55-61, 63, 65, 71, 75-76, 79, 84, 89, 97
Cook, Earl 114
Cothern, Hubert 104-105
Cowgill, John W. 111
Cross, Bill 63, 89
Cummings, Marvin 79
Cupelli, Ralph 10, 16, 26, 45 49, 50, 57

D
Davis, Jack 1-2, 11, 18, 24-26, 48, 51, 60, 62-63, 68, 72-74, 78, 80, 82, 89, 91-92
Davis, William B. 49, 55-57
Dille, Eugene 57
Divisions, American Infantry: 1st 45; 4th 31, 69-70, 74; 5th 8, 10-11, 15-16, 25, 29, 31, 32-34, 44, 47-50, 52-54, 56; 26th 73; 29th 42; 36th 129; 42nd 119; 80th 54; 83rd 91; 90th 41, 54, 121; 95th 54, 64; 103rd 26; 106th 66, 131-132; Airborne: 82nd 38, 67; 101st 38, 67, 71, 86, 122; Armored: 2nd 124-127; 4th 73; German Airborne: 3rd Parachute 47; 5th Parachute 47;
Drabek, Alex 87
Dunn, Kenneth 107, 128, 133
Dunn, Melvin Wallace; [Uncle Wallace] 3-14, 48, 53, 58, 60, 63, 68, 70, 73, 75-76, 79-81, 96-98, 101, 103, 105-106, 118, 128
Dunn, Ralph 127-128
Dunn, Robert 79, 90

E

Eisenhower, Dwight D. 14, 36-37, 67-68, 73, 83, 90, 123
England, Boyce 72-73

F

Faber Family, 31-32
Fields, James T. 111
Frankfurt, 33, 87, 89
French Forces of the Interior, 52
Forts, Benning: 54, 133; Bragg: 124; Gordon: 93; Hays: 24; Hamilton: 9; Knox: 34, 124; Leonard Wood: 103, 133; Leavenworth: 133; McNair: 133; Meade: 9; Meyers: 106; Sam Houston: 116, 132-133; Sill: 8, 16, 130

G

Garner, Jack 10
Gold Beach, 36, 39
Goebbels, Joseph 54

H

Haughey, Winfried 32, 53, 55, 90
Harris, Leo 55
Hawthorne, Virgil 77, 82
Hill, Blanche 101
Hill, 183: 29, 47; 383: 75; 386: 56-58, 60
Hitler, Adolph 38-39, 66, 91
Hyde, Junior 4, 9, 101, 103-104

I

Irwin, S. Leroy 70

J

Johnson, Robert 57
Juno Beach, 39

K

Karen, Fred 32
Kincaid, Walt 5
Knox, John 109, 111

L

Langfitt, Frank V. 23-24, 55, 90
Lemons, Ray 106-118
Liebner, Byron E. 16-18, 26-27, 45-46, 48, 71, 76, 77-78
Liebner, Lucille 19
Lindsey, Syd 2
Ludendorff Bridge, 85-86
Luxembourg, 2, 25, 31-32, 64, 66, 68-69, 74-75, 77, 80, 82, 96, 100

M

MacDuffee, Sandra 96-97, 100
Man of Confidence, 117
McNeill, Fred 6
Metz, 16, 54-56, 59-63, 75
Montebourg, 44
Mooseberg, 114-115
Mullins, Warren 62
Murphy, Wayne 7
Myrna Jean, 6

N

Neale, Robert 79
Niestein, 88
Normandy, 29, 35, 37, 42, 46-47, 50, 55

O

Omaha Beach, 37, 39, 41-43

P

Pas-de-Calis, 38
Patton, George 25, 35, 60, 67-68, 70-71, 73, 80, 84, 88
Pillboxes, 44, 64
Point-du-Hoc, 41
Purpleheart Lane, 60
Putscheid, 32-33, 78-80, 83

R

Redball Express, 53
Regiments: American infantry 2nd 55, 104; 10th 1-2, 8, 10, 15-17, 24-27, 30, 32, 44-47, 52-53, 55, 58-59, 64,

68-70, 73, 83-85, 89-92, 135-136; 11th 30, 54; 12th 74; 18th 45; 116th 42; 133rd 129; 179th 122; 222nd 119, 121-123; 232nd 119; 242nd 119
Renken, Lucille 18
Reims 53, 91-92
Rivers: Isar 115; Kyll 85; Main 49, 89; Meuse 53, 66; Moselle 54, 62, 85; Nims 84; Our 75, 78, 83; Prum 33, 84; Rhine 33, 65, 67, 83-85, 87; Ruhr 89-90; Sauer 32-33, 70-71, 73, 75, 83-84; Seille 52, 62; Seine 52, 83; Sure 83
Roosevelt, Franklin 63
Roosevelt, Theodore Jr. 41

S

Scala, Hector 111
Sicily, 46
Siegfried Line, 31, 54, 64-65, 83, 85
Silver Star, 25, 58
Stallbaum, Gerald 64-65
Stalags: Luft 1 111; Luft IV 111; VII A 114; 11B 105; Xlll D 113
Stephenson, Rachel 102-104
Stewart, James 107
Storey, Harold 2, 8, 19, 23, 46, 48-49, 55, 57-62, 64-65, 68, 71-72, 76-77, 93
Sword Beach, 39

T

Thomas, Leroy 32
Tibenham 107, 117-118
Tidworth Barracks, 10
Timmermann, Karl 86-87
Todd, Bob 61
Tucker, Tom 28-34, 60
Trench Foot, 59
Truman, Harry 114

U

Utah Beach, 19, 29, 36-37, 40-42, 44, 53

W

Williams, Art 80

www.ingramcontent.com/pod-product-compliance
Lightning Source LLC
Chambersburg PA
CBHW071724090426
42738CB00009B/1867